Booked for Life

The Bibliographic Memoir
of an Accidental Apologist

KARL KEATING

Booked for Life

The Bibliographic Memoir
of an Accidental Apologist

Catholic
Answers
Press

Published by Catholic Answers, Inc.
2020 Gillespie Way
El Cajon, California 92020
1-888-291-8000 orders
619-387-0042 fax
catholic.com

Printed in the United States of America

Cover design by www.ebooklaunch.com
Interior design by Sherry Russell, Russell Graphic Design

978-1-68357-059-2 hardcover
978-1-68357-060-8 paperback
978-1-68357-061-5 Kindle
978-1-68357-062-2 ePub

Contents

CONTENTS

Preface

I was twelve when my maternal grandmother came to visit, the second-longest trip of her life. (The longest was when she and my grandfather left the old country and settled in Chicago in 1908.) We moved to Southern California when I was six, so my childhood memories of her are few, but I have a photograph from her only visit to us. She sits in an overstuffed chair in one corner of the living room. The curtain is partly drawn, the room shadowed. Arms on wooden armrests, Grandma looks worn from a hard life raising eight children on the wages of a husband whose early working years were spent at a slaughterhouse. Two years after her visit she went into a hospital for the last time. When my mother returned from her good-bye trip, she said Grandma hadn't died of anything in particular but weariness and widowhood. From her bed she had said she was ready to join Grandpa, perhaps echoing John XXIII, who had said in his final days, "My bags are packed, and I'm ready to go."

When she visited, Grandma was given my bedroom. I was relegated to a cot in my parents' room. I remember lying there, the sun's warmth coming through diaphanous curtains. I delighted in the book I read, *The Borrowers* by Mary Norton. It had been published a decade before and was about tiny people who lived beneath the floorboards of a British house. They furnished their lodgings by "borrowing" things: a thimble for a table, a pocket watch for a wall clock, pins and needles for all sorts of uses. I can't recollect now what delighted me about the book. Perhaps it was the Britishisms more than the story itself. F. Scott Fitzgerald had said "the rich are different from you and me." The same might be said about American readers and English writers. I appreciated and liked the differentness from early on. That may have had a part to play in my choosing the five books that are the chief objects of discussion in this book. Their authors happen to have been English—except for Frank Sheed, who was born in Australia but did his chief apological work in England, so in these pages he will be considered an honorary Englishman.

At one time I thought of pursuing a degree program focused on John Henry Newman, one of the five, but never did. In anticipation of it I collected nearly all of his writings and many about him. Later I did some work toward a program focused on another English author whose complete works I have, Samuel Johnson. I have two large bookcases devoted to him, his writings, and his era. My other complete or almost-complete collections are of the works of Ronald Knox, Frank Sheed, and Arnold Lunn. So, all Englishmen (actual or honorary), all masters of the English language, all dedicated Christians. This emphasis on English writers came not in my adolescence but later, but perhaps an early impetus was the pleasure I took in the very English way that *The Borrowers* was written.

When I was a few years beyond reading that book I discovered that I excelled at mathematics. Robert A. Millikan High School had a math club. The members participated in tournaments held throughout Southern California, competing against as many as a hundred other schools at a time. A team consisted of five students, each focusing on a particular area of math or on a particular contest activity. I was comfortable with filling any slot except for one: I had an aversion to the chalk talk because the contestant had to make a presentation, in front of a panel of judges, on some abstruse mathematical topic. I was too shy to stand before such a panel. I chose one of the slots where all I had to do was to work out answers while seated at a desk. It was like taking a test in class.

Years later, as a Catholic apologist, I discovered I was comfortable speaking before large audiences, the larger the better. Small audiences proved awkward for me. I could speak before 2,000 people without anxiety but seemed to lose my way when speaking before twenty. Comfort returned when I spoke to just one or two at a time. Where others found a sweet spot between the intimacy of too few and the giantism of too many, I found a sour spot.

Our math club met under the tutelage of Helen Carter, a soon-to-retire teacher who took me under her wing. Years later, when I would drive up to Long Beach to visit my parents, sometimes I'd pay Mrs. Carter a visit. She lived with her sister in an older but handsome part of town. By this time I was engaged in apologetics, and we sometimes spoke about religion. She was Lutheran and seemed to have been brought up in a variant that inculcated a mild animus toward the Catholic Church. I was pleased to discover that she was pleased to discover, through our talks, that much of what she had been told about Catholics and their faith just wasn't so.

One of my recollections of her, before her retirement from teaching, was of her picking me up for a math tournament. I waited a block from home, at an easy-to-locate intersection. I thumbed through note cards, trying to memorize a few extra mathematical obscurities, thinking they might come in handy. One of them did. That day taught me the value of cramming. A contest question asked for the sum of a wide swath of integers, such as all the integers from 101 through 1001. On a note card I had jotted down the formula that allowed me to produce the answer within seconds. That day I won my section of the tournament, and our team won first prize overall. I was convinced that my street-corner cramming had made the difference, and it probably had, so closely matched were contestants otherwise. Cramming may not be an effective way to impart lifelong knowledge, but I discovered it works in tournaments.

That first year of high school I was at my apex. Our team participated in many tournaments, and I almost always finished at the top of my section, guaranteeing success to our team. I had grounds to imagine that I was the top tenth-grade math student in the whole of Southern California, and I likely was, but that year marked the end of my intellectual ascendancy, in math and everything else. Since then it has been a gradual decline to undistinguishedness.

I still have the James and James *Mathematics Dictionary*, which I read the way other people read cookbooks. It was a prize for winning an early tournament, and studying it allowed me to win subsequent tournaments. But that was half a century ago. When I open its pages now everything is in a language foreign to me. Although I may have lost the meaning of the text, I have not forgotten the joy of minutiae. What once prompted me to learn arcane mathematical formulas later prompted me to learn equally arcane theological formulas—probably not a result anticipated by James and James.

What Mrs. Carter was to me in mathematics, Robert Ciriello and William Marmion were to me in another field. They taught eleventh-grade American history in the team-teaching style. Each had a class of thirty or so, but regularly the classes were amalgamated with one or both of the teachers lecturing to the larger group. Throughout my school years I had good teachers, but Ciriello and Marmion were exceptional. I wondered why they taught high school rather than college. I feared their talents were wasted on many who sat around me. I owe the two a debt of gratitude I never found a way to repay. Through them I learned the evidentiary power of history, which, done properly, is far more than Leopold von Ranke's *wie es eigentlich gewesen*—"how it really was." History is more than a chronology, more than a catalogue of incidents. It is a window into the human condition, a playing-out not just of heroism and ideals but of private catastrophes and original sin.

When I came to write my first book, *Catholicism and Fundamentalism*, I realized that my authorities had to be limited if I were to win the minds of Protestant readers. I could not appeal to popes or councils or catechisms because they held no authority for "Bible Christians." I relied on the testimony of Scripture, history, and common sense, with the middle one often carrying the burden. On many matters—infant baptism is but one example—the sacred text can be interpreted multiple ways in good conscience. The historical record cannot. There is no ancient work that forbids baptism to children. There are several that refer to infant baptism not controversially but as an unexceptional, everyday occurrence. One of the powerful attractions of Newman's *Essay on the Development of Christian Doctrine* is his effectiveness in deducing what ancient Christians thought from how they practiced. People normally don't believe one thing and practice—however feebly or ineffectually—the opposite. They do not baptize infants while denouncing infant baptism. They do not disbelieve in the Real Presence while acting as though Christ were present on the altar. They do not render honor to a priest when they think he has no authority or role different from theirs.

My undergraduate studies—I majored in mathematics—were done at the San Diego campus of the University of California. At the time it was reputed to be one of the three top schools for math, the others being M.I.T. and Caltech. I chose UCSD over the others largely for financial reasons, tuition being only a fraction of what the better-known schools charged. It also had the advantage of being neither on the East Coast nor near Los Angeles, both of which were worth keeping away from, I thought.

I matriculated at the height of the campus disturbances. UCSD was home to Herbert Marcuse, idolized by the New Left, for which he served as theorist; today he is as forgotten as the Students for a Democratic Society, which disbanded in 1969. One of Marcuse's acolytes was a graduate student who would make her own name in a few years: Angela Davis. When I knew of her, she was the afro'd leader of one of the leftwing factions on campus and a regular rouser of rabble in the quad. Years later, in a moral and intellectual decline that eventually relegated her to obscurity, she ran for vice president of the United States on the Communist Party ticket. (She lost.)

A few friends and I started a campus newspaper called *Dimension*, an alternative to the far-left official school newspaper. We had great fun in skewering the pretensions of the disloyal opposition. Sometimes we did the skewering in ways other than in print. Once, the campus was in an uproar about some feigned indignity, one so important that I no longer can recall it. The leftists had protested at the chancellor's office, going so far as to throw rocks at the building, thus affirming the cogency of their arguments. But what should the next step be? Should further protests be held? That had to be decided through "participatory democracy," so a meeting was held in the cafeteria. A vote would be taken, but only after debate. Each side, the pro and the con, would be represented by two speakers. (This was the "participatory democracy" part.) First a New Left champion spoke in favor of escalation. Then someone spoke in favor of de-escalation. Then it was time for another pro-escalation speaker, but no one came forward. There was an awkward silence. The organizers were bewildered. There should have been no lack of students willing to urge their peers to further action.

Not seeing anyone rise to the occasion, I walked to the microphone. People looked at one another, wondering what was going on. They knew I was on the Right, not the Left. With mock enthusiasm I encouraged a vigorous attack on the chancellor's office. What fun we had at the first encounter, I said. How grown up we felt with our rhyming slogans. How satisfied we felt when pelting the building with rocks, especially when one broke a window and the chancellor's secretary was cut by flying glass. This was maturity! This was progress!

The room collapsed into paroxysms of laughter, and the vote was against further demonstrations. My first public talk had gone over well, and it probably has been the only time I have succeeded in turning a crowd from its initial purposes. That evening's success—less the success, actually, than the pleasure of confounding the other side—made me realize that arguments, even facetious ones, can be worth pursuing.

My undergraduate years were less productive than they ought to have been. My faithfulness to my major decreased as my interest in campus contretemps increased. I once had thought I would go on to a career in math, but now I was at sea. One day I returned to my apartment to find that my roommate had made a decision. He had been a computer science major but saw little future in the field—this was before the invention of the personal computer—and had concluded that his future should be in law. I confessed I didn't know what I could do with an advanced math degree, other than teach—something I was not inclined to do—so I, too, almost instantaneously, decided to apply to law school.

A few years later I found myself a member of the state bar with a solo law practice and few clients. I worked in an office so small some would mistake it for a closet. Over twelve years I built up my practice, though not as quickly as I should have. I had begun to engage in apologetics on the side, and ineluctably my avocation became my vocation. That wasn't my intention when I started dabbling in apologetics. I expected to practice law indefinitely, but apologetical delights kept popping up. I found that I enjoyed law, but I enjoyed apologetics more. In my last years as a lawyer I did little lawyering but much apologizing—in the religious sense. I closed my law office at the end of 1987.

Not many years after that I began attending the Catholic Rendezvous. The annual gathering, which took place over a long weekend, had been started by people associated with the long-defunct *Triumph* magazine, which had been founded by L. Brent Bozell, Jr., the brother-in-law of William F. Buckley, Jr. Bozell had written for Buckley's *National Review* for some years but by 1966 had concluded that political conservatism was insufficient for what ailed the West. What was required was an overt Catholic politics. Thus *Triumph*. The magazine never had a large circulation—opinion journals rarely do—and sputtered to its end, after a decade, because it alienated too many of its readers.

The Catholic Rendezvous brought together former staff members, writers, and readers, plus others, such as I, who were invited to attend for no apparent reason. The venue was the closed-for-the-season Ragamont Inn in Salisbury, Connecticut. The building dated from 1830 and looked it. I remember particularly the sloping wooden floors on the second story. I also remember an argument I walked into.

Warren Carroll, one of the founders of Christendom College, was in the kitchen. Facing him was a taller and younger man who ran a solo apologetics ministry out of his house trailer. He insisted that the only proper way to argue with a Protestant was to browbeat him, using insults if necessary. Carroll, who had a reputation for mild-mannered imperturbability, was perturbed. This may have been the only time in his adult life that he raised his voice and showed anger in public, but that seemed to be the only way to get the other man's attention.

That fellow I already knew by reputation, and over the next few years I had my own run-ins with him, though always at a continental distance, he living in New York and I in California. He relished arguing, but he thought arguing meant verbal fisticuffs. He gave his opponent no quarter and no respect, someone in error deserving no respect, in his mind. He insisted that he was the most effective Catholic apologist in the country and that only his system could show proven results. Eventually I asked him how many converts he had made. Like Fulton Sheen, he said zero, but he said it for a reason different from Sheen, who took no credit for the grace that worked through him to bring thousands into the Church. Sheen was being appropriately modest; this other man was just being honest. I suspected that his rude writings—he published a small-circulation newsletter—if they had any result at all, engendered sympathy for the Protestants he excoriated for disbelief and for the Catholics he excoriated more strongly still for having the impertinence to disagree with him.

By that time I had obtained an advanced degree in theology but, even while pursuing it, realized that most of what I would need for apologetics would have to be supplied privately. I would have to be self-taught, there being no formal, academic way to learn the craft. Not seeing what I needed in the present, I turned to the past, to the apologists of another era. I found them in books that gave me knowledge, confidence, and pleasure. I learned from them how to learn the Faith and how to understand it, how to defend the Faith and how to convey it.

The following pages are about those books and about their effect on me as I backed into apologetics. Whatever I have learned, I have learned from masters of the craft. I claim no novel insights, no fresh approaches. My goal has been emulation, originality being beyond my powers. I have been a Borrower, taking things from giants and repurposing what I have taken as needed. If this book enkindles in others the delight I found in these authors, my appropriation of their arguments and methods may find pardon for me here below and, perhaps, conviviality with them hereafter.

The Core of an Apologetics Library

In these pages I discuss and excerpt the five indispensable books that gave flesh to my apologetical aspirations. I have come to know them as one comes to know a good friend, and I have come to rely on them as one relies on a good friend. What follows are not book reviews but representative samples of these books' arguments and my reflections on those arguments, particularly as they influenced my development as an apologist.

On their own, the five form a rudimentary apologetics library. From them a prospective apologist will gain sufficient knowledge and skill to be of use to the Church. He will find himself able to answer most questions with intelligence and sympathy. He will learn what to do and, perhaps more importantly, what not to do when speaking to a crowd or to an individual. He will learn that apologetics is not gesticulations at a lectern or the regurgitation of verses, though it may involve standing behind a lectern and calling up verses. He will learn that *sola scriptura catholica* is not enough and that apologetics must engage not only the sacred text but history and other disciplines.

These books are arranged in a logical but not a chronological sequence. First comes a book that might be considered a precis of the others. It deals with nearly everything a Catholic apologist has to master, from knowledge of doctrines large and small to techniques used when dealing with hecklers at open-air meetings. *Catholic Evidence Training Outlines* is a period piece, but I know no book that does a better job of preparing apologists for their work.

This book was compiled by Maisie Ward and Frank Sheed from their years working with the Catholic Evidence Guild, so it seems appropriate that it be followed by my favorite Sheed book, *Theology and Sanity*. Ward and Sheed not only were apologists; they were publishers—and spouses. Their publishing house was called Sheed and Ward. Among its innumerable authors were Arnold Lunn and Ronald Knox, so I have placed books by those two next. At the end, entirely out of chronological order since it was the first written of all these books, is John Henry Newman's *Essay on the Development of Christian Doctrine*.

The five books can be read in any order, but they should be read more than once. Once through is not enough, just as once through a Bach concerto is not enough. Unexpected insights come the second or third time around. I hope the reader will gain from my storytelling, but I especially hope he will find delight in the extended excerpts and will be moved to acquire these books for his own library.

And then, interspersed among these five, there are twenty almost-indispensable books. These represent my best recollection of the other books that were the most important in my development as an apologist. Over the years my shelves may have lost, through inadvertence, one or two titles that ought to appear here, but that is unlikely. I superintend my books carefully and watch out for them—I am loyal to friends, whether animate or inanimate—and am neither a borrower nor a lender, at least when it comes to printed matter.

These twenty books are not ordered by their significance to me. I recall, for example, that the last on the list—Joseph Tixeront's *History of Dogmas*—was particularly instructive, and I spent much time with it. Quite useful, but with less time spent with it, was the first of the twenty, Nicholas Halligan's *The Sacraments and Their Celebration*. This is not to say I absorbed little from Halligan—after all, casting my eyes over hundreds of other books, this was one I chose as being among the most important to me—but it is a reflection of Tixeront's particular utility. Others that occupied much of my reading time were those by

Newman C. Eberhardt, Ludwig Ott, and Johannes Quasten.

Had I entered apologetics earlier or later, this list would be constituted differently. Five of these books first were published— or were republished after long being out of print—as I studied apologetics with some intensity in the mid-1980s. They came to my attention not because they had been part of the standard apologetical repertoire but because I stumbled across advertisements for them or reviews of them. Thus serendipity had a role.

What follows are not book reviews but acknowledgements of debts. I profited from all of these books, never had a way to extend my thanks to their authors, and hope to make up for that by recommending them to my readers. The most recent of these books was published more than thirty years ago now. Chronological snobbery might dissuade a few from taking them up, but then such people are not the sort to profit from books no matter when written. A few of these books remain in print; most have to be tracked down as a hunter might track down elusive prey.

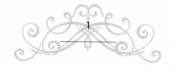

Catholic Evidence
Training Outlines

Maisie Ward and Frank Sheed

KNOW HOW TO DEAL WITH YOUR AUDIENCE

I begin with the book that likely had the greatest cumulative effect on me as an apologist: Maisie Ward and Frank Sheed's *Catholic Evidence Training Outlines*. I have the second edition, published in 1948. So far as I have been able to determine, Ward (1889–1975) was the chief author, but Sheed (1898–1982) contributed substantial portions of the text, some of which he incorporated into his later *Faith Comes by Hearing*. Ward already was well established as a senior speaker of London's Catholic Evidence Guild when Sheed joined the group. He bungled his first public appearance, the day being salvaged only when Ward got him down from the platform and won the crowd back. He was so impressed that he married her.

The first six paragraphs I quote here are taken from the introduction, "Street Corner Apologetic." The authors note that the Catholic apologist "faces a crowd which is almost totally apathetic: it retains a hostility to Catholicism, but a hostility from which all the sap has drained out." There had been a great change "in the space of ten years"—that is, 1938 to 1948. At the middle of those years was World War II. Wars have a way of changing public perceptions and interests in large ways, and Ward and Sheed perceived such changes.

The speaker's first problem, then, in the practical order is to gain [the crowd's] interest. He is no longer an object of interest merely *as* a Catholic. Their minds are not seething with questions on which they are conscious of bitter difference between him and themselves. To assume that they have an already-existent interest, only waiting to be exploited, in this or that doctrine of the Faith is to court failure. They have none such nor any awareness of the traditional lines of controversy. Allusion to old arguments, quotations of the texts of Scripture that have been flung back and forth for centuries, leave them unmoved because uninformed. These things make no impress on their minds at all, for there is nothing already there with which they may come into contact. If the crowd is to be interested in a doctrine now, it must be by the intrinsic interest of the doctrine, not by the quite extrinsic fact that non-Catholics used to fight about it. The convenient—but ultimately pernicious—interest which comes from controversy is no longer there. Protestantism is not what the speaker faces in the crowd but the Church's age-old enemy, inertia.

This paragraph was written literally before my time. It gave a snapshot of a period I could not know but one that was not distant from me. By the time I became interested in apologetics, 1948 was barely three decades in the past. I thought that things then could not have been all that different from what I was experiencing. I could tell that most people around me had little interest in religion, even those who obligatorily went to church on Sundays. I mean that they had no interest beyond the conventional. Churchgoing was just something that one did. Even the dutifully observant—in the Catholic context, those who went to Mass regularly and perhaps took part in some devotions—seemed not particularly interested in understanding the whys and wherefores of their beliefs, which they did their best to compartmentalize, usually successfully. (It was one thing to be seen praying the rosary in church; it was an eccentricity to be seen praying it in public. The sign of the cross might be made at the family dinner, but it seemed awkwardly out of place at a restaurant.)

> From this it follows that *proof has ceased to be the apologist's principal weapon*. Prove to a modern crowd that Our Lord instituted confession—they will simply say, "What if he did?" Prove that he was God—they will say, "What if he was?" Prove that the pope is not anti-Christ—they can but yawn and ask, "Who is, then?" Proof is always wasted on a man who is not interested in the question.

Every career is colored by time and place. No one entering apologetics today will encounter precisely the sorts of people I encountered, just as I came across people somewhat different in attitude or concerns from those encountered by the readers for whom *Catholic Evidence Training Outlines* originally was written. Ward and Sheed produced the second edition of this book after a military conflict that induced both existential despair and a heightened interest in Christianity. Within a decade the despair was largely dissipated, but so was the superadded interest in religion. Things had gotten more or less back to normal, certainly in the U.S. but also in much of Europe. Years later still there came a revivification of "Bible Christianity," something the authors likely could not have anticipated.

What I found, in my early work, was that proof indeed was my "principal weapon," because the people I commonly dealt with in those years—Protestants with decided views about their own faith and decided prejudices about Catholicism—were eager for proofs. Perhaps I should say they were eager for *disproofs*. They wanted to see Catholicism proved wrong, as they already presumed it to be. When I engaged with them, they challenged me to bring forth proofs about my religion. I realized even then that such people were not the norm. They were not representative of the bulk of the population. Most people indeed were disinterested in proofs because they were disinterested in questions. People who don't seek answers don't care about proofs.

Two things are needed that a man may be moved by proof. First he must understand quite clearly what the thing is that you are trying to prove. Secondly he must realize that it is important—and important for *him*. And in practice there is a third. He must want it. Once he wants it, he will be prepared to accept the proof if the proof is good. Indeed, once he wants it, he may want it so badly that he refuses to waste time over the proof, and it might be the proponent's duty to *insist* that he examine the proof. Proof, then, for the present-day Catholic apologist, has gone into comparative eclipse. It simply will not do the work. What will?

The answer is, of course, exposition. We have already said that for proof to move him, a man must understand what the thing means that one wants him to accept. The whole effort of modern street corner apologetic is directed toward this in overwhelming proportion. Instead of laboring away at one or the other of the proofs that there is a God, devote nine-tenths of that energy to making the crowd realize what we mean by God and the remaining one-tenth, at the end of the process, to the proofs. If a man does not know—really solidly know—what you mean by God, what is the use of proving to him that there *is* one? What is the use of proving that Christ was God? Or again, if a man does not grasp with his whole mind the meaning and importance of revealed and certain truth, what have you gained by providing to him that the Church is infallible? Or, to take one other example, if a man does not know what virginity *means*—not simply as a definition but in all the immense richness of what it signifies and implies as to the whole meaning of life—what is the use of establishing that Our Lady was a virgin?

I never have been a street-corner apologist, literally or figuratively. I suppose that has been a consequence of temperament. Proof I have had some facility with; exposition, not so much. I find it easier to respond to a polite question or to a heckler's challenge than to work up a talk that can turn a disinterested crowd into a crowd leaning forward to catch the next bit of exposition. But I understood from the first what was being said here, and I knew that the greater need was to spark that initial interest, without which not much else could follow. In raw numbers, there were far more people who were disinclined to think about the Faith than there were who wanted to fight about it, but I was attracted to the latter—as I said, probably due to reasons of temperament, theirs and mine.

The work, then, of showing what a doctrine means is the speaker's principal occupation on the platform. And this, as I have suggested, is more than a matter of definition. It involves showing what the doctrine implies, what things flow from it, not simply how it works (though that is of great importance) but what richness of truth is folded up in it, what light it casts upon God or man or nature.

Thus the speaker is taking care of the two things already suggested as requisite if a man is to accept: he is showing what the doctrine means and what its importance is. He is also taking care of the—practically—necessary third, that the hearer should come to want it. For the fact is that truth will make a better appeal for itself than any propagandist will make for it. It is not by our tribute to doctrines that men will normally come to desire them, not because we say they are splendid that men will come to see their splendor. Just as attempts by us to prove that doctrines are true tend to arouse opposition, to remind the hearers that there is another side, so attempts by us to paint the attractiveness of doctrines tend to arouse suspicion, to remind the hearers of other men who have tried high-pressure salesmanship upon them. Summarizing, then, this first section: the Guild speaker's direct work is to make his hearers see what the doctrines are, not to see that they are true nor to see that they are desirable, but to see *them*, and, because they *are* true and good, the doctrines will set about their own effort to capture the man, for God who made them true and good endowed man with faculties whose object is truth and goodness.

Catholic Evidence Training Outlines divides its instructional material into two. Thirty-three short chapters are for "junior speakers," and forty-eight are for "senior speakers." All of the earlier materials need to be mastered before a student can graduate to the more subtle later material. Sandwiched between the two courses are nine "technical lectures." I found them the most useful part of the book because they dealt with the *how* rather than with the *what*. I profited from every page, but by the time I came across *Catholic Evidence Training Outlines* I already had worked up arguments on most of the topics addressed in the junior and senior courses. I felt particular weaknesses in the public application of what I knew: how to convey the material to listeners or readers.

THE MENTAL OUTLOOK OF A CATHOLIC STREET CORNER APOLOGIST

Qualities both of the intellect and the will are necessary for the work.

1. The will.

> (a) We are servants of the crowd and must therefore give our very best. This means individual preparation for each lecture. Speaking unprepared becomes very easy after a time, but it is a temptation to be resisted fiercely. A poor speaker doing his best is quite literally much better than a brilliant speaker doing his second best.

Fulton Sheen was known for his facility with extemporaneous remarks, particularly on his 1950s television program, *Life Is Worth Living*. Viewers marveled at his ability to speak coherently and movingly, for half an hour, without reference to notes. That was the impression, but it was not the reality. Sheen later remarked that his habit was to write out his remarks, reduce them to note cards, and then memorize the note cards. A consummate dramatist, Sheen knew that content and delivery should go together. The best content, if packaged poorly, will make little impression on an audience.

Few people will read a book with an unattractive cover because the cover disinclines them from ever picking up the book in the first place. We may be advised not to judge a book by its cover, but most people do, and that suggests that publishers should not be satisfied only with well-manicured text; they also should ensure that the text is presented in a pleasing way. So it is with public speaking, whether on television, on radio, or at an open-air meeting in Hyde Park's Speakers' Corner. Even abstruse themes, such as the Trinity, can be made accessible if a speaker does sufficient preparation—something he should do anyway, even if only out of respect for the crowd.

I once listened to a recording of a Catholic-versus-Protestant debate in which the Catholic speaker was a former employee of the apostolate I founded, Catholic Answers. I no longer recall the topic of the debate, but I recall with discomfort his opening remarks. The debate was held in Queens, New York, and the Catholic, who lived a few states away, had a considerable drive to get to the venue. His first words to the audience were an apology for his lack of preparation for the debate. He said that, in the weeks leading up to the debate, he had been too busy to work up his remarks and so, as he drove northward, he scribbled notes on a yellow legal pad whenever he stopped at a traffic light or pulled over for a break.

His remarks that evening were from those hastily written notes—and it showed. He had not done the audience the courtesy of preparing. That would have been obvious as he fumbled through his disordered yellow sheets—no three-by-five cards or memorized points for him that night—but I found it especially imprudent for him to reveal to his listeners how little he regarded them. It is one thing not to prepare well and to have your lack of preparation show itself as you move through your talk. It is something else to begin your talk with an acknowledgement that you didn't have enough consideration to prepare.

> b) We must try to like the crowd—even those members of it who most obviously do not like us. We must not be resentful if they find us dull and uninteresting. We probably are. Nor must we feel a sense of grievance if they misbehave. They did not invite us to come and talk to them.

I never found myself disliking a crowd as a crowd, though there have been times when I have felt no fondness for some members of a crowd. Only a few times have I been interrupted while speaking, usually to my advantage. Most people, even those who disagree strongly with a speaker, believe in courtesy. To their minds, a speaker may be quite mistaken in his thinking, but he deserves the chance to state his positions without interruption from hecklers or the omniscient (who are usually the same). Those few times when I have been interrupted—invariably by a young male standing at the back and unwilling to identify himself—have worked in my favor because interrupters never are as knowledgeable about an issue as they imagine; their arguments don't persuade the audience of anything, though their demeanor persuades it of their crassness. The result is sympathy for the speaker and a more attentive audience.

> (c) Sarcasm is always a grave offense. The speaker must never hurt a questioner's feelings. Never sneer. Never raise a laugh at someone's expense. If a joke is made at your expense, do not be annoyed. If it is a good joke, enjoy it.

I have had good jokes made at my expense—bad jokes too—and I have made jokes at other speakers' expense when at conferences with multiple speakers. The jokes about me I generally have appreciated. I can't say whether my jokes about other speakers always have been appreciated by them, though the audiences seemed to like them.

(d) Absolute honesty is the rule always. Never pretend that a doctrine or fact is other than it really is. *Above all* never pretend to know what one does not know.

This is a point I tried to emphasize to apologists who worked with or under me. There is no loss of face in admitting one's ignorance of some doctrinal issue, and the Church suffers no harm when we acknowledge personal and corporate failures in Catholic history.

Early on I learned that an admission of ignorance humanizes a speaker. An audience is filled with people who, on the topic under discussion, are ignorant in greater or lesser degrees—usually greater, which is why they have come to listen to the speaker in the first place. For a speaker to admit not knowing something (this normally occurs in the question-and-answer session following the talk) immediately brings him down to earth in the mind of the audience. It makes the rest of what he says—that part with which he seems to speak with authority or, at least, studied knowledge—more convincing, not less.

I never came across a Catholic apologist who tried to "pretend that a doctrine or a fact is other than it really is." Well, a doctrine, anyway. Some Catholics and many non-Catholics misconstrue Catholic doctrines, and some less-than-faithful Catholics present doctrines as they wish they were rather than as they are, but those are not things done by any apologists of my acquaintance. More common is the tendency to smooth rough historical edges. The impulse is understandable but should be avoided. A speaker's discomfort with some episode of history usually indicates his insufficient study of it.

(e) We are licensed by our bishop to speak not as individuals but as members of the Guild. We have no other *locus standi* than as Guild members. This involves obedience to rule and, what is more trying, to officials. If by chance one has a grievance against Guild officers, it is well to remember that one is not doing the work for their sake. In any society officers are a necessary evil, but no less necessary for being an evil.

(f) Do not resent criticism. You are not expected to like it, but there is no progress without it.

(g) The work *must* have a background of prayer. The Guildsman should aim at spending as much time before the Blessed Sacrament as he spends on the outdoor platform.

A lifetime ago, apologists may have been "licensed" in some more or less formal way by their dioceses, but that formality fell into desuetude about the same time as kissing episcopal rings. Just as well, in both cases. Although a certain arm's-length oversight from the chancery makes sense—no bishop wants anyone speaking on behalf of the Church to come off as a crackpot, either in content or in style—there is an unexpressed acknowledgement that apologetics, at least since Vatican II, has become a lay activity. It once was the exclusive domain of the clergy. When the Catholic Evidence Guild was established in 1918, a layman speaking in public on a Catholic theme was an oddity, and it was odder still for a layman to speak controversially on a controversial theme, particularly in a predominantly Protestant country such as Britain. With most apologetics now being done by laymen, bishops seem to prefer a less intrusive oversight, the better to claim dissociation from offenders, if necessary.

2. The intellect.

(a) The prime virtue in a teacher is lucidity. Avoid long lectures. No crowd can hold more than a twenty-minute lecture in its head at one stretch. Avoid long, difficult, or technical words. A word the crowd does not understand is wasted. Avoid lines of thought that are too difficult. Be concrete, use illustration plentifully. Do not try to be "eloquent." Eloquence and lucidity are sworn foes.

My experience has been with fifty-minute talks because that is the length most hosting organizations, whether parishes or conferences, expect. The twenty-minute lecture proposed by Ward and Sheed may have been best for an outdoor venue where a speaker hoped to build an audience from people who otherwise were on their way to someplace else, but at a parish or hall, where listeners can sit in relative comfort and, free from distractions, are more able to follow a speaker's argument, a lengthier talk is warranted—but not too lengthy.

I used to speak annually at a particular conference where fifty minutes was the time allotted to each speaker, to give the audience a chance to stretch or leave the room between presentations that began on the hour. One of the most popular speakers, a man invited back year after year, was a professor at an East Coast college and the writer of many short and delightfully phrased books. He never once kept to the fifty-minute limit. Each of his talks was ninety minutes long. Each time he spoke, he threw off the conference schedule for that day. Gentle remonstrances from the organizers were ineffectual. Each year he ignored frantic timekeepers, who held up signs indicating his time was out, and each year the lunch break and afternoon talks were pushed back. (He commonly spoke late morning, flying in early that day and flying home immediately after his talk.) At length the organizers stopped inviting him. It took me some years to realize why he persistently spoke for ninety minutes: his remarks—always read from a prepared text—were really chapters from upcoming books, and all his chapters were the same length.

> (b) Teach positive truths. Waste no time demonstrating that other religions are wrong. Teach Catholicism. Be quite clear what it is you want to teach.

I have followed this instruction only halfway. In my talks and in my books I often have tried to demonstrate "that other religions are wrong" because that was what I was hired to speak or write about. *Catholicism and Fundamentalism* was an exposition of

Catholic teaching and history in light of Fundamentalist attacks. It would not have been possible to refute those attacks without explaining why they were wrong—and why Fundamentalism, to the extent it differs from Catholicism, is wrong. But I understand the point made by Ward and Sheed. If the topic for an outdoor presentation is the Eucharist, it is enough to explain what we understand it to be; there is no need, in the allotment of twenty minutes, to explain why impanation is a wrong theory.

(c) Try to show the crowd each doctrine not only as it is in itself but in its relation to other doctrines. See the teaching of the Church as a *totality* and try to convey it so.

(d) Do your best to understand the particular crowd you are talking to, and arrange your teaching in relation thereto. One crowd is not exactly like another. Ask yourself very carefully whether the lecture you have prepared is likely to be of any use to the crowd. Watch them carefully and see what they are making of it.

HOW TO DEVELOP YOUR IDEAS

1. Reading.
Not an enormous amount required. Reading with a pencil, the result a jumble of facts and texts and phrases.

The Catholic Evidence Guild's training program worked in small increments. A junior speaker would learn how to discuss one narrow point and then would stand in front of the class and give a brief talk. The class would act not just as audience but as hecklers, to whom the speaker would have to respond in a coherent way. Once the trainee learned to do this with several topics, he was permitted to appear in public, but only on those topics. As he learned how to handle additional items, he was given more and more liberty, until finally he graduated from the junior program and became a senior speaker, at which point he could initiate public presentations and likely had to oversee upcoming junior speakers.

A speaker's education came partly in the classroom but largely at home. He was expected to do enough reading to master a topic. That might take ten minutes or it might take ten hours, depending on the topic. First came the gathering of information, usually inchoate. Then came the digesting and organization.

For me there was no analogue to this system. When I began in apologetics, I knew no apologists. The Catholic Evidence Guild still existed—across the Atlantic. That did me little good. I was forced to improvise. I did what research I thought was necessary for the topic but often enough discovered, in the heat of a post-lecture discussion, that I had overlooked entirely certain key elements. I tried to learn from not knowing. The learning came exclusively from reading, there being no alternative for me. "Not an enormous amount required," said *Catholic Evidence Training Outlines*. That may have been true in London but not in San Diego.

2. Digesting.
You must have a thorough understanding of your matter in itself and in its relation to all things else. It must be pondered over and gazed at from every standpoint. You must make it yours,

(a) Historically in its foundation and development.

(b) In relation to the rest of Catholic doctrine.

(c) In its present working.

Analogy of London, which can only be understood in its relation to England, in its historical development, and in the work it does.

(a) Foundation and development.

Scripture: some texts (and contexts) must be known thoroughly. Get very clearly what was in the mind of our Lord or the apostle whose words you use. With reverence one may ask *Why?* (Also notice apparently contradictory texts.)

I suspect I felt relief when I first read this: "some texts (and contexts) must be known thoroughly." The operative word was *some*. There was no expectation here that an apologist would have most of the Bible memorized—or even all the passages useful in apologetics. My mind often has seemed more a sieve than a trap. I have appreciated that some speakers, Catholic and Protestant, could conjure up at will substantial segments of the sacred text. I never had that ability, no doubt because I never tried to cultivate it, on the premise that there were better uses for my time.

I read accounts of nineteenth-century American plowmen who, as they repetitively turned over furrows, each day added several verses to memory until, by their middle years, they had captured the whole text of the Bible. (These seemed always to be Protestants who memorized the Authorized Version. I never heard of a Catholic memorizing the whole of the Douay-Rheims.) I would have been more inclined to memorize the poetry of Belloc, Frost, and Eliot—something I didn't do much of either.

Despite my disinclination to memorize, I suppose I ended up with more memorized verses than Ward and Sheed had expected of their charges. How could a professional apologist not? Has any Catholic ever engaged in apologetics without knowing Matthew 16:18–19? Has any ever spoken of creation without quoting Genesis 1:1? Well, maybe those verses are among the "some."

Development: you must know what attitude the Church adopted at different stages of its history, when she defined, when she might seem not to have laid so much stress and *why?*

(b) Its relation to the rest of Catholic doctrine.

In all this you have been working on your idea, and seeing its birth and growth you have almost inevitably a clearer view of the doctrine as it stands now. But Catholic doctrines are not a collection of oddments flung together like curios in a pawnshop window. They are not even like books arranged alphabetically or in some other convenient way on the shelves of a library. They are a family related to one another by the closest ties: you must study your idea in its setting, in its relation to the whole body of the Church's teaching.

Look on the Church's teaching as a countryside of which you are able to take a bird's-eye view. First you see the great dogmas like the great centers: the Trinity, the Incarnation, original sin and free will, the immortality of the soul. Then you see the smaller towns: confession, the priesthood, matrimony. And smaller still the villages, roads between, from which the life pulses out, while even the smallest village in the Church's countryside gives something to the greatest metropolis.

You must then know each doctrine in its relation to the mass. In your mind it must not be isolated, since it gains vastly in meaning from its position.

(c) The doctrine in action.
Having thus seen the doctrine in its birth, its growth, and its varied relationships, you must now see it in action. And to do this fully you must ponder on

(1) Its effect on yourself.

(2) Its effect on your crowd.
In (1) be very thorough in thinking out just what it means to you and what the effect on you would be of the loss of it.

In (2) try to imagine what difference it would make to your non-Catholic listeners if they accepted it, and to do so thoroughly you must realize that in its place they either have something or nothing.

Consider carefully and honestly the objections that have been brought up against the doctrine.

You may now claim to have for practical purposes mastered your idea. You can toss it from hand to hand. You can set it down, walk round it and look carefully at it. You can look at it from above or turn it upside down and look at it from below. You know where it is likely to arouse opposition and where it is likely to make an appeal. In short, it is yours.

In this section, *Catholic Evidence Training Outlines* encapsulates what I aimed for in my private preparations: to know a doctrine from all angles, particularly knowing it as it was seen by those who opposed it. Just as one entry in the James and James *Mathematical Dictionary* would send me to another, which sent me to a third and, at length, back to my starting point, so with my doctrinal studies. Considering an objection to doctrine A led me to research doctrine B, which in turn brought up objection C. Sometimes I passed through a dozen ancillary issues before returning to my starting point. Most of those ancillary issues I never made public use of, but the exercise helped me understand why non-Catholics (and even some Catholics) objected to particular teachings of the Church.

3. Arranging.

(a) Our job it not to *utter* a message. It is to *deliver* a message, to deliver it to people—to people who either are determined not to receive it or who at best will not make any effort to receive it. We have to persuade them that something is essential which they have managed to do without all their lives. So that we must remember that we have not only to prove our doctrines (which means a lecture) but to convey them to people (which means a speech).

We must ask ourselves always some such questions as this: "Even if the crowd believe all that I am saying is true, will it (given the state of their minds) make the slightest different to them?"

(b) People are extremely human—quite as human as we are—and the human mind can only with profit receive one thing at a time, so that it is definitely necessary to make our speech concern itself with one subject only. We should be able to express the exact object of each speech in one sentence.

The dangers to which we are liable are talking of everything and talking of nothing at all. One may hold a crowd by sheer personality and give them nothing.

(c) Simple words must be used. The crowd do not know words like "finite," "infinite," "Immaculate Conception," "Judaism," "impeccability," "contrition," etc.

Here again I distinguished my situation from that of Ward and Sheed. They wrote in terms of speaking in Hyde Park, but I spoke in organized parish or conference venues. I could rely on my audiences having a better, if only slightly better, grasp of words of art than the people strolling through Speakers' Corner on a weekend afternoon. Also, having fifty minutes rather than twenty, I had the time to define at least a few terms, among them *impeccability* as distinguished from *infallibility*, a term often abused by opponents of the papacy.

(d) The lecture must be short, not more than twenty minutes. We must have one idea and a plan, simple and vertebrate (and thus easy to remember). It must have

(1) A beginning: make contact with the crowd mind.

(2) A middle: every point must be concerned with the

thing to be shown. Keep summing up at intervals and make each point follow inevitably.

(3) An end: summing up the whole and restating the position.

(e) Do not learn by heart. Learn your plan as a matter of four or five points (each to occupy four or five minutes) and know exactly what you wish to say on each point. But when giving the lecture have the whole of it in mind all the time. Concentrate on the point you are on, but be aware of all that you have said and all that you mean to say.

At this point the apologist mimics Fulton Sheen, not in delivery or knowledge but in knowing his subject well enough that he can speak without notes, at least in theory. Few Catholic apologists have attempted to do so. For a long time I resisted. In the earliest years I wrote out my remarks completely and highlighted key words. Having the full text gave me an escape route. If my mind went blank, I could put my head down and just read—not the best approach dramatically, but I kept in mind that John Henry Newman and Ronald Knox always preached from prepared texts and made no effort to make eye contact with their listeners. They managed not to be driven out of the ambo, and I thought that, *in extremis*, I could manage not to be driven off the dais if I found myself reduced to reading my remarks. I never actually had to do that, except for a paragraph or so, until I recovered my pace and the outline of my talk came back into my mind.

At some point I ceased having on hand the full text of my talk and relied on a detailed outline, one that might extend over two pages. The first and greatest advantage was that I no longer had to fear dropping a sheaf of papers and discovering, after I had rearranged them on the lectern, that I had gotten them out of order and that my talk was going in circles. The second advantage was that I was freed from reliance on my text. I felt no compulsion to read through several paragraphs that didn't seem to be making an impress on the audience, fearing I would have wasted those paragraphs if I hadn't used them. It is easy to skip over a bullet point in an outline but not so easy to skip over a page of printed text.

Eventually I reduced my notes to a single page and often enough found myself hardly referring to it. That was true particularly when giving talks on the Fundamentalist attack on the Faith. After having given more or less the same talk ten or twenty times, I found that I needed the notes only for when my mind went inexplicably blank. This is the reason a good musician will have before him at the concert the score of a piece he has memorized thoroughly. If all goes well, he will not need to refer to the score at all. If his mind and fingers have a momentary lapse, a quick glance at the score will let him get on track without an awkward interruption of the flow.

Late in my apologetical career I took an entirely different approach to the preparation of talks: I wrote down nothing at all. Whereas in the past I first wrote a rough outline, then the full text, then an outline to be used at the lectern, now I did none of that. I "wrote" in my head. Usually I began with a historical incident relevant to my theme. I worked up a mental paragraph or two, often finding that the right words came surprisingly easily when trying to compose a narrative. This small segment I repeatedly "spoke" internally (imagining I was speaking in public) until, after modifications that seemed to come of their own volition, the words became fixed. Then I moved outward from there, working up the immediately preceding or following material.

I discovered that with this method, which made my remarks more a story than a speech, I was able to focus more on delivery, no longer having to worry about following the content on note sheets. I never have excelled at speaking, though at times audiences were as generous to me, out of charity, as they had been, out of justice, to more competent speakers. Unlike some other speakers, I have not been blessed with a good voice or good stage presence. I never review videos of my talks out of worry that I would find them so discouraging that I would give up public speaking altogether. But I did conclude that my late-career method of preparing a fresh talk ended up, on average, producing something that both in content and delivery was superior to what I had been able to produce before.

ON RELATING SPEECH TO MIND OF LISTENERS

1. Crowds in general have no conscious interest in religion. This fact is the source of two problems facing the Catholic speaker:

(a) *How to get them to listen at all.* Unless they are interested, they walk away. One solution is to start with something remote from the subject but certain to interest them—some topic of public concern, or even a funny story, or a string of them—in the hope that they will listen when the real subject of the speech at last arrives. These things can be useful, but they do not touch on the second problem:

(b) *How to make any permanent impression even upon those who listen.* Unless the doctrine taught can be built firmly on to something already existent as an abiding interest in their minds, it will not remain. The speaker should strive more and more to discover these deeper interests and be less and less dependent on the useful but definitely cheaper methods mentioned under (a).

In my early years of public speaking, I occasionally included a "funny story" in my remarks, to get the audience's attention. Once—and only once—my execution of a joke was so effective that I got a standing ovation that went on for several minutes, but that was an outlier. Usually a joke would receive polite laughter that died down quickly. Not by nature being a jokester, I soon enough switched to mild wit, which I found appropriate to insert at multiple places in a talk, not just at the beginning. Partly I took a cue from Thomas Howard, author of *Evangelical Is Not Enough*, whose wit-laced lectures I long had admired. I thought his talks used wit particularly well and never heavy-handedly.

2. Every doctrine and practice of the Church contains some such common ground—that is, there is something in every one of them which is also to be found in the human mind at large. The two remaining problems then remaining, when one is preparing a speech on any doctrine, are:

(a) To discover some very powerful crowd interest which is also operative in that doctrine.

(b) To discover how the one may be hooked on to the other.

3. Discovering the common interest.

If the subject is

Confession: every human being is interested in sin.

I don't suppose Ward and Sheed intended this line to be taken in two ways. Or perhaps they did: indeed, "every person is interested in sin," both as a topic and as a pastime. Over the years I have given a little thought to writing a book called *Favorite Sins*. I suspect it would sell well, just based on its title.

(b) Infallibility: everyone is in the most hopeless muddle about life—its meaning, purpose, rules—and at least dimly aware of it.

(c) The saints: people are obsessed by the problem of suffering.

The class-taker should vary the examples from his own experience. He can do this by choosing other topics, and, even on the subjects here given, other grounds of interest are to be found.

4. Using the common interest.

Take the common ground, discuss it so that they can recognize themselves and their interest. Show them how the thing, whatever it is, stops short in their mind and lies there incomplete. Then show how perfectly the Catholic doctrine fits on. For example, confession. Show how the confessional psychologically *fits* sin:

(a) While pleasant in contemplation and in action, sin is usually stale and musty to look back on. One seldom gets pleasure but rather distaste out of the memory of past sins. The confessional therefore, which involves putting the sin into words, is the exact antithesis of the sin and makes sin look its least attractive.

(b) Sin is an assertion of self. The confession to a man is a corresponding snub of self.

(c) Sin is a fascinating subject, but the fascination is sterile. The contemplation of other people's sins—e.g., in newspaper and cinema—leads to nothing, but the contemplation of one's own sins in the confessional can lead to a rebuilding of character.

(d) Sin while in appearance is always an assertion of self is in fact always a diminishing of self.

There are literally scores of openings on this line. At all times the speaker must be asking himself the one question: what human interest am I using as my starting point, trying to build something permanent on to?

HOW TO HANDLE A CROWD

1. Our object is to secure that each person that hears us shall carry away with him the greatest possible amount of

Catholicism in thought and in action. We therefore summon to our aid the "crowd" habit, knowing that, if we do not, it will be used against us.

2. A disorganized mass is not a crowd. Ten men may be, and a thousand men may not be, a crowd. A crowd is formed by a community of interest, by the turning of feelings and thoughts in a common direction. Individual self-consciousness and certain ordinary limitations disappear, some emotions and faculties are reduced, and others are reinforced and exalted. The business of creating a crowd consists in providing the common channel of interest as quickly as possible. Hecklers are a great help throughout but particularly in the preliminary steps towards creating a crowd.

I wish I'd had the chance to speak at Speakers' Corner. Never did I experience oratorical rough and tumble of the sort one commonly could see there, where it might take a speaker several minutes, bantering with passersby, before he had a crowd to give his talk to. Whenever I spoke to more than a handful of people, it was at an organized event, and even when the event was hosted by non-Catholics that meant general civility. The one exception was a debate I had with a minister from Iglesia ni Cristo (Church of Christ), a sect from the Philippines. The audience of 3,500 consisted almost entirely of adherents to that religion. When I first sat at my table in front of the audience, a man pulled up a folding chair and sat beside me. I asked him who he was. He said he was a bodyguard and was there to protect me in case irritated members of his sect stormed the platform.

3. Learn to talk *to* them, not simply to talk in their presence but literally *to* them. This is one of the most difficult of all arts to acquire.

4. Once a crowd is formed we proceed by repeated blows to drive deeper the original impression made. Repetition, clear

statement, concrete affirmation, conviction are the qualities to aim at here. Humor (well-controlled) can be useful but should *not* be aimed at. Aim at being yourself—at personality. All technical skill in speaking is only a way of "freeing" personality. Build up a real human relationship with the crowd. Feel absolutely at home. Plain, above-board, even downright methods are required. "Be cheap yet deep." Choose your own line and do not be put off by hecklers. The speaker must be the leader of the crowd. Self-mastery in all its forms is essential. Avoid too much overt reasoning. But you must have done it before speaking yourself, and your handling of your subject must be equal to any logical test that may be applied.

5. What kind of materials can they take? The best subjects (i.e. those which provide the best channel of "crowd" interest) are those which appeal to the common elements in human nature. The method of handling largely governs the capacity of absorption of the crowd. (A really competent speaker can give them philosophy.) Generally speaking the subjects that appeal best may be classified as:

(a) Those that appeal to the individual personality— "massive" subjects that influence the whole man.

(b) Things that lead to action—"What must I *do* to be saved?"

(c) As a development of (a), subjects or groups of subjects that have a wide appeal—"Catholic" subjects.

In preparing your speech be very rigid with yourself. Ask "Of what use is all this to anybody—particularly to the body I am going to talk to?" Unless you know the answer to this question, you might as well stay at home.

6. How much of a subject can the crowd absorb? The fatal error is trying to give too much. Indigestion is a mental, as

well as a physical, fact. Wise breaks, humor, variety, topical-ness, on the part of the speaker all increase the capacity of the crowd. A great weight of suggestion must be behind all our work. We must aim at causing future thought in our audi-ence, as well as an immediate effect.

An audience that goes away understanding a few points has been better served than an audience that goes away with many undigested points. In my earliest talks I tried to handle issues as thoroughly as I could. If the issue was Scripture-based, I cited multiple verses to prove my point. I may have impressed listeners with my apparent command of the Bible, but I left them unable to replicate the argument when speaking with others. If my goal was to equip them to argue on the issue, I failed by giving them too much. I learned to focus my argument to them so they could convey its substance to others.

7. Finally, summing up all, *Be interesting.*

QUESTIONS AND INTERJECTIONS

1. This is almost the most important part of our work and certainly the most difficult for beginners. The only safe foun-dation for answering questions is to have in our own minds a big constructive picture of the Church to which we refer all separate points of doctrine and in which all details (with which questions are mostly concerned) fall into their proper place. We must not allow ourselves to be dragged into wran-gling on minor points, chopping texts, etc. Remember irrel-evancies in a lecture produce irrelevant questions.

I appreciated the spontaneity and unpredictability of ques-tion-and-answer sessions. After a few years I realized I seldom was getting any fresh questions, having fielded the same ones over and over. In that I suppose I was like a confessor who, after a while, seldom hears of a fresh sin—and perhaps just as well. I do recall vividly a question that I received once and knew instantly that I never would receive again. At the conclusion of a public debate a young woman approached the microphone. She said she was not a Catholic but her grandmother, who lived in Mexico, was. The grandmother, she said, had a large hairball that she kept in a jar under her bed, and she worshiped the hairball. Why did the Catholic Church encourage that? The question took me by surprise. It was not one I had found addressed in any of the books by my favorite apologists, but I think I managed to produce a sufficiently satisfying reply.

(a) Always give a lecture. Usually keep question answering to the end of the lecture (unless you are trying to collect a crowd). Interjections should normally be left alone.

(b) Make up your mind whether to answer the question or not.

(1) Is it on your subject? It generally is better not to take totally irrelevant questions, but if no other question can be got, it may be well to do so.

(2) Is the questioner sincere or insincere? It may be difficult to decide. In either case it is usually better to answer—for the sake of the crowd, even if the questioner does not listen to the answer.

(3) Do you know the answer? If not, admit it candidly. The world will not come to an end.

If pride goeth before a fall, this is where apologists—at least those just getting started in apologetics—tend to stumble. You wish to appear omnicompetent, but you find yourself asked something you should know but don't know, in front of an audience eager for an answer. The temptation is to maneuver like a politician trying to explain an unpopular stance. The simplest thing is the best thing: admit ignorance. Some will be disappointed—"Well, so much for *his* skills!"—but most will appreciate your candor and will give all the more credence to whatever else you say.

(c) If you decide to answer:

(1) Repeat the question. This ensures that the crowd will follow the whole discussion.

(2) Never let the thing be a purely formal cut-and-dried matter. You are not answering a question *but a questioner.*

(3) Therefore find out what the question means to the questioner. Be deliberate and leisurely about this. Converse with the questioner, yet so as to make the crowd listen. Frequently the questioner asks what he does not mean, simply through not knowing Catholic terms—e.g. Immaculate Conception.

(4) Find out not only what the questioner wants to know but try to get at what is the real trouble in his mind. Detailed questions nearly always involve some more fundamental error. Thus a man who questions the virginity of Our Lady probably does not see any value in virginity. One who objects to the infallibility of the pope probably does not really believe God has given a revelation or sees no value in certain truth.

(5) Answer with the utmost simplicity. Normally the crowd take a long time to hear what you are really saying. One must be prepared to give the same teaching again and again, each time trying to be clearer than the last.

(6) Do not let questioners rush you from point to point. Do not pass on to the next question until you have either made the crowd see the answer to the one you are on or come to the conclusion that you cannot get them to see it.

(7) Above all avoid mere argumentation. Never let the thing degenerate into a squabble between yourself and the questioner. Make the crowd realize that it is not a case of him against you but of him against the Universal Church.

A squabble can be amusing, so long as you're an observer and not a participant, but I have yet to witness an apologetics squabble that had a good result. A speaker who succumbs to emotion is a speaker who has lost the confidence of his audience and therefore has lost the overall argument. Perhaps I've lucked out. I've faced testy questioners, even hecklers, but never people whose goal was to disrupt rather than dispute.

The Sacraments and Their Celebration

Nicholas Halligan

There are seven sacraments but seventy times seven ways to misunderstand them. Given enough time, a Catholic apologist will imagine he has been presented with each of those misunderstandings. It takes being confronted with only a few to alter the course of one's career.

My first overt apologetical act was undertaken nearly forty years ago. I exited Mass one Sunday to discover anti-Catholic flyers on the windshields of the cars in the parish parking lot. The flyers excoriated the Mass and the priesthood.

I no longer remember my initial reaction, but probably I was less annoyed with the Church being attacked than I was with the attack being done so obtusely. This has been my attitude concerning attacks for as long as I can remember, so I presume it was my attitude then. I do not expect non-Catholics to endorse the Church or its teachings. If they did, they would be Catholics. I do not expect them to understand Catholic teachings or practices; people rarely learn about things they are predisposed to have no interest in. But I do expect active critics of the Faith to know something about the thing they criticize, yet many of them act like book reviewers who have not read the book they intend to slam or film critics who have not watched the film they propose to demolish.

The flyers left on the cars annoyed me sufficiently that I wrote a counter-flyer of my own. The anti-Catholic flyers had been distributed by members of a Fundamentalist church only a mile from my parish. Turnabout being fair play, a few Sundays later I placed my flyers on the windshields of the cars in that church's parking lot. Done with the first of the spiritual works of mercy—instructing the ignorant—I stood across the street to see what would happen. When the morning service ended, first out the door were the deacons or elders; they spotted my flyers and began to pick them off the cars, but they were not fast enough. Most congregants went home with something extra to read.

That incident was the launching of Catholic Answers, though I did not at the time imagine that anything of consequence would come from my escapade. My purpose was to correct the errors of a single anti-Catholic flyer, and even then I expected little. I did not expect Fundamentalists to alter their religious allegiance based on anything I had to say, but, if they were going to reject Catholicism, I wanted them to reject the actual thing and not a caricature of it. You don't believe in the existence of a sacrificial priesthood? Fine, but don't reject it on the notion that the priesthood arose from Mithraism or that priests use the confessional to ferret out information with which to blackmail penitents. You don't believe that in the Mass Christ becomes literally present under the appearances of bread and wine? Fine, but don't reject the Mass based on its supposed pagan origins. If you wish to reject the Catholic faith, reject it for what it is, not for what it is not.

The anti-Catholic flyer attacked two sacraments, holy orders and the Eucharist. I suppose only limitations of space prevented similar attacks on the remaining five sacraments, though even the Fundamentalists who composed the flyer may have found it awkward to come down hard on baptism and matrimony, which they accepted, though as "ordinances." I learned soon enough that Fundamentalists see sacraments—or ordinances—as symbolic and nothing more. Catholics may chuckle to learn that many "Bible Christians" find ways to reinterpret the Last Supper's use of wine, some going so far to insist that the wine really was indistinguishable from the grape juice found in any supermarket. But even those Fundamentalists who concede that Jesus and the Twelve drank wine insist that that was all they drank, that the wine did not literally become something more profound. "This is my blood" must be understood as "This represents my blood," a representation that could have been made as usefully with grape juice or any other drink.

I came across *The Sacraments and Their Celebration* at a convenient time. It was published just as I was writing the newspaper series that would become *Catholicism and Fundamentalism*. The clarity and concision shown by Nicholas Halligan (1917–1997) helped focus my mind as I labored in the evenings to work up my response to anti-Catholic complaints about the sacraments. Particularly useful was his section on sacramental validity. What does it take for a sacrament to be valid, to "take"? Often less than one might guess.

"From the practice of the Church it is certain that no disposition or intention is required of infants or the perpetually insane to receive validly the sacraments of which they are capable: baptism, confirmation, and even orders and the Eucharist. Having no personal sin, they need no personal act to be justified, and, being unable to cooperate in their own salvation, the intention of Christ and the Church through the will of the minister suffices or supplies for them." The point here is not that an infant or insane person is going to be ordained but that some sacraments "take" even absent a positive will on the part of a recipient who is incapable of having such a positive will.

But those are exceptional cases (aside from infants presented for baptism, of course). An otherwise competent adult must have an intention to receive a particular sacrament. It must not be "a passive attitude, neither willing nor not willing. . . . The intention must be at least habitual and may be implicit, except for orders, matrimony, and the Eucharist (not for Viaticum), when it must be explicit." (Some will be comforted to know that it thus is not possible to be married inadvertently.)

Considerations such as these were of more use to me than to anyone I ever discussed the sacraments with. I can recall no one ever confiding to me anxiety about whether he had become married through inattention or ordained by mistake, nor did anyone ever ask me whether an insane family member could be confirmed. I suppose most priests never come across such worries either. But Halligan's dissection of the sacraments helped clarify in my mind things I already knew or, at least, suspected about the sacraments, and that gave me a certain level of comfort when writing or speaking about the seven ordinary means for the transmission of sanctifying grace.

Radio Replies

Leslie Rumble and Charles M. Carty

The opening line to this series' preface has been quoted so often by so many that few people realize its provenance: "There are not over a hundred people in the United States who hate the Catholic Church. There are millions, however, who hate what they wrongly believe to be the Catholic Church—which is, of course, quite a different thing."

The writer was then-Msgr. Fulton Sheen, who continues,

> These millions can hardly be blamed for hating Catholics because Catholics "adore statues"; because they "put the Blessed Mother on the same level as God"; because they say "indulgence is a permission to commit sin"; because the pope "is a Fascist" [keep in mind these books appeared in 1938]; because the "Church is the defender of capitalism." If the Church taught or believed any one of these things it should be hated, but the fact is that the Church does not believe nor teach any one of them. It follows then that the hatred of the millions is directed against *error* and not against *truth*. As a matter of fact, if we Catholics believed all of the untruths and lies which were said against the Church, we probably would hate the Church a thousand times more than they do.

Eight decades ago, that may have been an effective way to introduce a set of three books comprising several thousand questions and answers concerning nearly every aspect of Catholic belief, history, and practice. Today those words seem stilted and imprecise. If all these charges levied against the Church were true, would Catholics hate the Church "a thousand times more" than those outside the Church? Not likely. Most of them simply would cease to be Catholics and would give the Church as little concern, and as little animosity, as they give to other organizations to which they don't belong. Even in 1938, that line of Sheen's likely was taken as overwrought.

His first line, though, has had a life of its own. One catches its cleverness immediately: "you don't dislike us for what we are but for what you mistakenly think we are." My own experience in apologetics has shown that to be the case often enough, but Sheen's words obscure a brutal fact: if not in 1938, certainly today there are millions who hate the Catholic Church even though they do understand what it is and what it teaches. It is Catholic teachings they hate, particularly moral teachings, and so they hate the messenger.

When Sheen wrote, there persisted that Protestant anti-Catholicism that stretched back to the Reformation and would stretch forward to my own time, even if in attenuated form. Back then, even non-Christian opponents of the Church accepted, however imperfectly, Christian anthropology and Christian mores. They may not have believed in the Fall, but they unconsciously admitted its consequences. Anti-clericalists opposed what they perceived to be the venality and rapacity of clerics, but they did not much oppose the moral principles and understanding of human nature that the clerics were assigned to transmit. That largely has changed in an era in which people of seeming intelligence are unsure what constitutes a human being and what their own identity might be.

Sheen continues his preface with a line that resonated with me: "If I were not a Catholic and were looking for the true Church in the world today, I would look for the one Church which did not get along with the world; in other words, I would look for the Church which the world hates." This remains a good guide. The Church is to be in the world but not of it, which means the Church and the world always will be in tension.

I never have been tempted to leave the Church, though often enough I have left the company of Catholics who have annoyed me. If, through some sudden intellectual disability, I decided to leave the Catholic faith, I suppose I would seek repose in repose: I would end up outside of any active practice of religion. I could no more see myself becoming a Methodist or Baptist than I could see myself becoming a member of some made-in-America sect. One of the disattractions of those other churches is that no one outside of them opposes them or hates them. They are not alive enough for anyone to wish them dead. The intensity of opposition to the Catholic Church makes that Church attractive because it implies that Catholic teachings are true.

All that being said, I found *Radio Replies* useful because, even fifty years after Rumble and Carty brought out their books, many of the questions that had been posed still were being posed. In the early years of my career I dealt more with Fundamentalists than with theologically liberal Christians or with unbelievers. The Fundamentalists had imbibed their anti-Catholicism from writers and preachers who flourished when *Radio Replies* first appeared. Such people may not have been as commonplace as they once were—similarly for their prejudices—but they were commonplace enough that I found it necessary to work up answers to questions that never would have come up in any Catholic course of study. I found those questions in *Radio Replies*, from which I constructed the earliest formulations of my answers.

The three volumes were cobbled together from material used on Fr. Leslie Rumble's "Question Box Program," which aired on a Sydney radio station. His first volume consisted of 1,588 questions and replies. Charles M. Carty was an American priest who "was carrying on as a Catholic Campaigner for Christ, the apostolate to the man in the street through the medium of [his] trailer and loud-speaking system." He said that Rumble answered "the questions I had to answer before friendly and hostile audiences throughout my summer campaign." *Radio Replies* proved to be "a handy standard reference book of excellence for popular questions which are more than ever being asked by restless and bewildered multitudes."

Carty purchased copies of Rumble's book, and it became the most popular thing on his literature table. It also became to be too expensive to keep in stock, so he arranged to republish the book—and, later, its sequels—in the United States. Thus his name, too, became attached to *Radio Replies*, even though the replies were the work of Rumble.

Father Rumble (1892–1975) came from a confused religious background. His family was Anglican. When he was sixteen, his father unexpectedly became a Catholic and insisted that his whole family do likewise. Rumble acquiesced reluctantly but after two years returned to Anglicanism. When he was twenty-one he rejoined the Catholic Church and began study for the priesthood. Shortly after that Rumble's father announced that he had quit the Church of Rome and, with the rest of the family, had returned to the Anglican Church. "For ten years father and son maintained a controversial correspondence," recounts the *Australian Dictionary of National Biography,* until, just before young Rumble was ordained, his father and the rest of the family became Catholics once again.

Rumble was ordained in 1927 and began teaching theology. In preparation for a Eucharistic congress he began a weekly question-and-answer radio program that continued until 1968. "Rumble's knowledge of the varieties of belief (derived from his family's experience) conditioned him to play fair with questioners, whom he always treated as honest inquirers. Using plain language and short sentences, and avoiding rhetoric, he spoke ninety words to the minute in a voice like worn sandpaper, giving an effect of common sense and rationality. When anyone asked what the Church taught about a specific subject, he quoted the Bible—thus quietly claiming it as the book of the Church. He liked to bring in Protestant authorities to support a case and kept the works of many Protestant authors on his shelves."

I was pleased to learn of Rumble's "voice like worn sandpaper"; it was comforting to know that his success in defending the faith was not a function of a mellifluous voice. That knowledge, though, came to me decades after I first came across *Radio Replies*. From the first I saw the books' utility. What I particularly learned from them was the effectiveness of candor. Rumble made no effort to hide the blemishes of Catholic history, and he offered no excuses for Catholics' moral or intellectual failings. He just laid out the facts, and the facts took care of themselves. It was the winsomeness and plainspokenness of his short replies that made them convincing. I tried to learn from that.

Faith Comes by Hearing

Frank Sheed

"This is the successor to *Catholic Evidence Training Outlines*," Sheed begins. The earlier book was written chiefly by his wife, Maisie Ward, though his name, too, appears on the title page. *Faith Comes by Hearing* was written by Sheed alone. The earlier work went through multiple editions and twenty impressions, and "it was used by thousands who spoke under cover, in lecture halls and forums and classrooms, and even in pulpits." But times had changed.

By 1967 the Catholic Evidence Guild was nearly moribund. It still sent lecturers to Speakers' Corner, but the robust give-and-take of the twenties and thirties had been muted by the turbulent sixties. The world had become noisy, said Sheed: "television and radio and mass-circulation magazines, newspapers full of wars and the possibility of worse wars." The old style of public apologetics—particularly in the form of public lectures given before crowds that were hostile to, or at least suspicious of, the Church—was not as effective as it had been.

In earlier times,

> A Catholic speaker faced an audience of which practically every member had a solid and stateable—and stated— set of anti-Catholic prejudices. There were usually two sections. One held that the Catholic Church put the Virgin Mary in the place of Christ, used images to the violation of the Second Commandment, and went to confession instead of going straight to God. The other section accused the Church of denying man's animal ancestry and of thinking that the world was made in six days. Both sections united in the view that the Church was hostile to virtue, intellectual freedom, science, and the nation.

This actually made the situation easy for the Catholic apologist. "He knew what specific things the Church was accused of, and by defending and explaining her attitude on these points, he was certain of holding the interest of the crowd. There was no risk that the crowd would be bored. One had merely to stand up in a public place and say the word 'confession.' The crowd would do the rest."

But 1967 was not 1927. First of all, there were few crowds. In the old days, particularly in England but also in other places that the Catholic Evidence Guild was active, street-corner preaching was commonplace, there being few other ways of communicating publicly. By the time television had matured, that no longer was so. In the process, even the crowds—to whatever extent there still were crowds—changed too.

> The Catholic then faces a crowd not deeply interested; it may retain a hostility to Catholicism, but a hostility from which all the sap has been drained out. It is a hostility without vehemence and without shape—a slight discoloration marking the place of what was once a great wound. They do not hate the Church as an enemy of God—which is a mistaken but very stimulating view—nor as a teacher of false doctrines. What they have is simply a mistrustful feeling that they do not quite know what she is at and that her existence somehow comports a threat to their own individual and national liberty.

In the course of forty years the Catholic speaker had ceased to be an object of interest in merely being a Catholic. This was not his fault. It was a consequence of a change in the listeners. A kind of non-intellectualism had become prevalent. Once, people of all and of no persuasions seemed interested in knowing and in disputing what could be known; that appeared to be less so in the disruptive decade in which Sheed wrote.

He was writing long after the acme of the Catholic Evidence Guild's work. He had witnessed the slow but persistent change in

the Guild's audiences. In the early days the Guild's listeners consisted mainly of diehard old-line Protestants who thought of the
Catholic Church as the Whore of Babylon and of diehard old-line
materialists who seemed trapped in the philosophical amber of the
nineteenth century. By 1967 that had changed. There remained
members of each group, but the edges largely had worn off. The
crowds now—to the extent there were crowds at all, open-air
gatherings no longer being as fashionable as they had been—were
less pointed in their opinions. Most listeners, although willing to
listen, did not come with presuppositions or with the prejudices
that once made such events lively. They had become sedate in
their ideas and their manners. *Catholic Evidence Training Outlines*
included material on how to handle hecklers. There is no parallel
material in *Faith Comes by Hearing* because there no longer were
many hecklers. The art of heckling had fallen on hard times.

I profited much from *Faith Comes by Hearing*, though I profited
more from *Catholic Evidence Training Outlines*—not just because
the latter was much longer and appealed to me in its structure
and intent but because, by the time I came across *Faith Comes
by Hearing*, the situation in the field had begun to change again.
Old-line "Bible Christianity" was making a comeback. So was
old-line materialism, though its rise would become most notice-
able later with the advent of the New Atheists. In 1967 hardly
anyone would have imagined that within two decades Fundamentalism would be resurgent. Fewer still would have imagined
that the materialism of their great-grandfather's era would reappear in modern dress.

Sheed elsewhere noted that you can't prevent men from drawing
true conclusions from true facts. It is just as accurate to say that you
can't prevent them from dredging up errors of the past and imagining that the errors are novelties. Eighteen centuries ago it seemed
that Gnosticism had been vanquished, but the heresy returned in
multiple guises, such as the New Age movement, in the twentieth century. The epiphenomena change; the essence persists. That
is why apologetical techniques of 1927 that may have seemed not
quite pertinent in 1967 could become pertinent again in later years.

Winning Converts

John A. O'Brien

In "How You Can Win Converts," the second of the four chapters contributed by this book's editor, the reader is instructed to use "casual contacts." An example is given. "Some years ago I drove into a filling station. Noticing a stranger standing by the gas pump, I said to myself: 'I'm going to see if I can land this soul for Christ.'" Fr. John A. O'Brien (1893–1980) struck up a conversation on desultory topics and then asked the man "if he would be interested in seeing a new altar which we had recently erected." O'Brien took him to the nearby parish, showed him the altar "but also the whole church, with its stations, paintings, statues, and stained glass windows." Finally he showed him the confessional, about which, he opined, the man probably had heard stories. "Plenty" was the reply. O'Brien opened the door, invited the man to look inside, and explained how a confession was conducted.

After that, "I invited him to an inquiry class which had just gotten underway," even though the man was to be in the city only two weeks. That turned out to be enough. The fellow returned to his hometown and later sent O'Brien a telegram: "Just received my First Holy Communion. Am the happiest man in the world. Many thanks."

Even though I'm not a priest, I easily enough can imagine replicating most of what O'Brien did. I'd have no trouble showing someone around a church, explaining the accoutrements, giving an overview of the Mass as well as of confession, answering the usual objections raised by "Bible Christians" or by those of no religion. Where I would have trouble is Step 1. I've never been a "hail fellow well met" person. I don't think anyone ever has applied the adjective "gregarious" to me. Once I get in a conversation, I can keep it running. The difficulty is with the ignition switch.

Not so my friend Rosalind Moss, one-time apologist at Catholic Answers and convert from Judaism but now in religious life as Mother Miriam of the Lamb of God, O.S.B. Years ago, several of us headed off for a cruise sponsored by the apostolate. After retrieving our luggage at a distant city, we piled into an airport van that would take us to our hotel. The only other occupants were a young couple, beside whom Ros sat. The others and I slid into the rear seat. Just before we pulled away from the curb, Ros leaned toward the driver and asked where he was from. He said he was Haitian. "So, you're Catholic?" she asked, with a bit of upturned Yiddish emphasis on the last word. He seemed taken by surprise and just nodded. "Don't you just love being Catholic?" she continued, elongating the verb. He nodded again, watching her in the rearview mirror.

I glanced at the young couple. They looked perplexed and uncomfortable. I suppose the rest of us looked bewildered. Could we have done what Ros had done? I, at any rate, didn't have the chutzpah even to try, let alone to get away with it. Coming from me, such questions would have seemed an imposition; coming from her, they were reassurance to the driver and an indirect invitation to the young couple.

Winning Converts is subtitled "A Symposium on Methods of Convert Making for Priests and Lay People." Published in 1948, its twenty-one chapters, written by eighteen contributors (all priests, except for Clare Boothe Luce), are among the most uplifting I ever have come across—and also, inadvertently, among the most dispiriting. Let me make an analogy.

McGuffey Readers were the primary textbook for much of America—rural America in particular—during the final two-thirds of the nineteenth century. The six chief volumes were intended for children in grades one through six, after which most of the pupils would leave school to work on the family farm or elsewhere. The sixth of the books, intended for twelve-year-olds, provided readings from, among others, Milton and

Shakespeare. Nowadays, many students get through college having read no Shakespeare and having never even heard of Milton. William McGuffey's *Readers* thus show, simultaneously, how poorly educated contemporary students are and how well educated the generality of students could be, if only their education were pursued in a better way.

So it is with *Winning Converts*. The book presents stories of great success in making converts: hundreds of them each year, for decades running, in a single parish, even in such unlikely places as (heavily Baptist) Harlem. The successes are a rebuke to what passes for convert-making in an age, such as ours, that is welcoming enough to converts who find their own way to the church door but can't be bothered to go into the highways and byways to invite them in.

John E. Odou, a Jesuit priest in Southern California, writes about "information talks" intended for the curious. "Catholics are not allowed to attend unless they bring a non-Catholic. It is difficult to keep Catholics out, because they seem to be interested in knowing more about their own faith. However this is the danger that faces information talks. It can easily become a Catholic group and be transformed into a study club. To avoid this mistake it is wise to keep the number of non-Catholics proportionately greater than the number of Catholics."

James F. Cunningham, who was the superior general of the Paulist Fathers, notes that dealing with rural folks is not always easy. He counsels against speaking, on the first night, on "Why I Am a Catholic" or on the Virgin Mary—two good topics, but not for the lead-off talk. "In our first week too, we found that the larger part of our audience did not like the music we were using—classical numbers and Catholic hymns. They wanted hillbilly music and their own hymns." Be all things to all men, advised St. Paul. In Decherd, Tennessee, they "brought out well in excess of 700 on the third night, and the whole population of the town was only 850. Again we had to get used to being called 'Mister' and 'Brother.' Yet no offense was intended; we were as surprised to be called anything other than 'Father' as they were to see us preaching in cassock and mission cross."

In other parts of the country prospective converts may be more inclined to learn through reading than through preaching. "The convert should be given considerable reading matter according to his intelligence, both books and pamphlets, and they should all be given *free*," insists then-Msgr. Fulton J. Sheen. "The pamphlet rack in the back of a church should have the money box taken out of it, and all the pamphlets should be given gratis. If you wanted to know something about Communism, the Communist headquarters would send you a subscription to the *Daily Worker* free, and flood you with literature, but when a non-Catholic wants to find out about the Eucharist, he has to pay a dime."

When I was arranging for Catholic Answers to reprint *Winning Converts*, I was able track down the last surviving contributor, Fr. William J. Quinlan, who had been ordained in 1938. He said he "always had been a street man," going house to house, looking particularly for Catholics to bring back to the Church but also for non-Catholics to bring into the Church for the first time. "Evangelization is getting out and knocking on doors." Then eighty-two, he said he often felt like not going on his rounds—"I'm tired, or it's dark"—but he recognized that "there's someone who's been waiting for me every time." His is a spirit little seen in clerics today. Similarly with a comment made by another contributor, Paulist priest John T. McGinn: "The writer takes the view that the American clergy are vividly aware of the necessity of a more systematic and energetic apostolate to the non-Catholics of our country." If McGinn were alive today, I suspect he would recast that sentence.

Although I never found myself able to replicate what the writers of *Winning Converts* accomplished, their words boosted my desire to practice apologetics in whatever way I found myself capable. I discovered early on that I was capable in some things and incapable in others. Whether, with time, the balance shifted in my favor I can't say, but I remain acutely conscious of whole acreages which I have had no success in plowing. It's a comfort to remember that even St. Paul failed to move some hearts and minds. Often, no matter how universal our ambition, the best we can do is to be some things to some men.

Theology and Sanity

Frank Sheed

THE FAITH CAN BE EXCITING IF YOU PRESENT IT RIGHT

If there is a chief fault of this book, it is its title. At first glance—
and at second glance, for that matter—*Theology and Sanity* suggests itself to be a book about psychology and its relation to
religion. Frank Sheed gets past that in the first few pages. By
sanity he means recognizing that God is and that he is everywhere; *insanity* is the denial of God and his omnipresence—it's
the denial of half of reality and the more important half at that.

> My concern in this book is not with the will but with
> the intellect, not with sanctity but with sanity. The
> difference is too often overlooked in the practice of
> religion. The soul has two faculties, and they should be
> clearly distinguished. There is the will: its work is to
> love—and so to choose, to decide, to act. There is the
> intellect: its work is to know, to understand, to see. To
> see what? To see what's there.

I learned early on that, to many people, this is a revolutionary
idea: that the human soul has two faculties, intellect and will,
and that their functions are distinct yet complementary. Few
people think about thinking as distinguished from willing. The
distinction just never occurs to them. They find themselves
stymied when trying to understand what the human person is and
how he operates. I learned that beginning with the basics can be

like sharing the most hidden secrets of the universe. Once people grasp such elementary distinctions, whole worlds open up to them.

The late Fr. Ray Ryland, long-time chaplain at Catholic Answers, told a story about a fellow priest-professor who taught at a nominally Catholic college. That professor wanted to attract students to his new class and decided to title it "Underground Catholicism." In the class description he promised to reveal the deepest secrets of the Catholic religion. The labeling worked, and the class was over-subscribed. Week after week the professor regaled students with unimaginable tidbits about Catholicism. They delighted in what he revealed to them, and he delighted in never revealing to them that all he was doing was teaching from the *Baltimore Catechism.*

Seeing God everywhere and all things upheld by him is not a matter of sanctity but of plain sanity, because God *is* everywhere and all things *are* upheld by him. What we do about it may be sanctity, but merely *seeing* it is sanity. To overlook God's presence is not simply to be irreligious; it is a kind of insanity, like overlooking anything else that is actually there. . . .

God is not only a fact of religion. He is a fact. Not to see him is to be wrong about everything, which includes being wrong about one's self. It does not require any extreme of religious fanaticism for a man to want to know what he is, and this he cannot know without some study of the Being who alone brought him into existence and holds him there. . . .

The first difficulty in the way of the intellect's functioning well is that it hates to function at all, at any rate beyond the point where functioning begins to require effort. The result is that when any matter arises which is properly the job of the intellect, then either nothing gets done at all, or else the imagination leaps in and does it instead. There is nothing to be done with the intellect until imagination has been put firmly in its place. And this is extraordinarily difficult. One of the results of the Fall of Man is that imagination has got completely out of hand,

and even one who does not believe in that "considerable catastrophe," as Hilaire Belloc calls it, must at least admit that imagination plays a part in the mind's affairs totally out of proportion to its merits, so much out of proportion indeed as to suggest some long-standing derangement in man's nature.

Consider what imagination is. It is the power we have of making mental pictures of the material universe. What our senses have experienced—the sights the eye has seen, the sounds the ear has heard, what we have smelled, touched, tasted—can be reproduced by the imagination either as they originally came through our senses or in any variety of new combinations. A moment's reflection upon what life would be like if we lacked this power will show how valuable a part the imagination has to play, but it is a subordinate part and entirely limited to the world of matter. What the senses cannot experience, the imagination cannot make a picture of.

But in the state in which we now are, this picture-making power seems able to out-shout almost every other power we have. It is so commonplace that it can storm the will. The will may have decided firmly for sobriety or chastity: the imagination conjures up the picture of a glass of beer or a girl, and the will finds its decision wavering and breaking. But our concern is not with the effect of imagination upon the will but upon the intellect. There is practical value in dwelling a moment on this unpleasant business.

I pass over the damage imagination does to our thinking by way of distraction, because the experience is too poignantly familiar to need emphasis. Time and again we set out upon a train of abstract thought and come to ourselves at the end of an hour with the sickening realization that for the last fifty-nine minutes we have been watching imagination's pictures flash across the mind and the abstract thinking is still to do. Yet bad as that is, it is not the worst of the ways in which imagination hinders the functioning of intellect, because we are aware of our unhappy tendency and, when the urgency is great enough, can take steps to control it. But it has two other ways of interference, very dangerous because we do not suspect their danger or even their existence, and very important in our inquiry because they operate most powerfully in the field of religion.

The first of these is that the imagination acts as censor upon what the intellect shall accept. Tell a man, for instance, that his soul has no shape or size or color or weight, and the chances are that he will retort that such a thing is inconceivable. If we reply that it is not inconceivable but only unimaginable, he will consider that we have conceded his case—and will proceed to use the word "unimaginable" with the same happy finality as the word "inconceivable." For indeed in the usage of our day, the two words have become interchangeable. That they are thus interchangeable is a measure of the decay of thinking, and to sort them out and see them as distinct is an essential first step in the mind's movement toward health.

Words are a problem, particularly for those unskilled in making distinctions. Just as "unimaginable" and "inconceivable" are taken to mean the same thing, so with "inerrant" and "infallible" when the topic is Scripture and so with other pairs of words that impede useful discussion because many discussants don't know how to distinguish between them. Consider "soul" and "spirit." Every living thing has a soul, which is its life-giving principle. The souls of animals and plants are material principles; they die when the animals and plants die. (Rocks have no souls and so have no life.) The human soul differs markedly from the souls of the lower orders because it is spiritual, not material. It is a spirit, not matter. When a human body dies, the human soul perdures because spirits can't die.

This seems commonsensical enough when stated this way, but it generally is not something listeners have given thought to. This can generate confusions when an apologist speaks on the assumption that his terms are understood. It's not a case of I say *potayto* but you say *potahto*. It more a case of I say *potayto* but you hear *tomahto*.

To distinguish them we must distinguish spirit from matter, and this distinction is worth a little space here because it will be vital at every point of our inquiry. We shall return to it many times; this is only a beginning. Of spirit we have already spoken as lacking the properties of matter. But it would be a poor definition of anything to say of it simply that it is not something else. If all one can say of a thing is that it is not some other thing, then in the absence of that other thing one would not be able to say anything of it at all. But spirit would still be something even if matter did not exist, and we cannot feel that we have made much advance in our knowledge of spirit until we can speak of it thus in its own proper nature.

Spirit, we say, is the being that knows and loves, and this is a positive statement of its *activity*, what it does. But we can say something also of its *nature*, what it is. Briefly, *spirit is the being which has its own nature so firmly in its grasp that it can never become some other thing.* Any material thing is in the constant peril of becoming something else: wood is burned and becomes ash, oxygen meets hydrogen and becomes water, hay is eaten and becomes cow. In short any material thing is what it is, but tenaciously. My body, being material, might be eaten by a cannibal, and some of my body would be absorbed to become his body. But my soul can never thus be made into something else. The reason is bound up with a truth we have already mentioned—that material things have constituent parts, and spiritual things have not. What has parts can be taken apart. Because material things have parts, molecules and such, these parts can be separated from one another and made to enter into new alliances with other parts similarly separated from the company they had, until that moment, been keeping. But a spirit has no parts; therefore it cannot be taken apart. It can exist only as a whole. God might annihilate it, but, while it exists, it can only be what it is. It can never be anything else. Worms will one day eat my body but not my mind. Even the worm that dieth not finds the mind too tough to consume.

This is simple philosophy, but it is simply marvelous to those who hear it for the first time. Few people ever give much thought to what spirit is. For that matter, they don't give much thought to matter's underlying nature either. Aquinas tells us that a spirit is a simple thing, simple in the sense of not being made of parts. If spirit is simple, matter is complex. Just to say that goes against common experience: what we see around us seems comfortable to us. A mountain is large, but we can grasp it in our minds. But spirit? We accept that spirit exists—that spirits exist—but most of us are at a loss to say much about spirit, precisely because it seems difficult.

Our perception, then, is that the simple thing is difficult and the complex thing is easy, which is true to an extent, if by that we mean that the easy thing is something we don't have to apply mental labor to and the difficult thing is something our mind has trouble mastering. All that said, the distinction Sheed makes between matter and spirit is a revelation to people who never thought about the question. They are further surprised when, a bit later, they are told that they just now have been "doing" philosophy.

> What has parts, then, can cease to be what it is and become something else: that is one limitation from which spirit is free. But there is another. What has parts can occupy space—space indeed may be thought of as the arrangement matter makes to spread its parts in. It is from the occupation of space that those properties flow which affect the senses. That is why matter does. That is why spirit does not.
>
> We may now return to the distinction between "unimaginable" and "inconceivable." To say that something is unimaginable is merely to say that the imagination cannot make a picture of it. But pictures are only of the material world; and to that, imagination is limited. Naturally it cannot form pictures of spiritual realities, angels, or human souls, or love or justice. Imagination cannot form mental pictures of these, because none of our senses could experience them. To complain that a spiritual thing is unimaginable would be like complaining that the air is invisible. The air is beyond the reach of one particular sense, namely sight, because it lacks color. Spirit is beyond the reach of all

the senses (and so of imagination) because it lacks all material qualities. With the eyes of your body you cannot see justice. You can see a just man or an unjust man, but justice you cannot see with your eyes. Nor can you hear it or smell it or run it across your palate or bark your shins on it.

Imagination naturally plays a large role in artistic depictions of the spiritual or supernatural. This usually has a happy result if the artist is Bernini or Michelangelo, but lesser artists often enough produce works that fail to speak to many observers. Sometimes bad art overpowers good will. I never have had much of a devotion to the Sacred Heart, for example, because I never have been able to get past the poor artistry of traditional depictions of our Lord with his heart aflame. Those depictions, treacly and seemingly invented to appeal to feminine sentiments of a certain era, leave me cold and have conspired against an easy adoption of the devotion. Only once did I come across an artistically fine representation of the Sacred Heart, a rendering at once manly and comforting, but that was so long ago that I have forgotten where I saw the image.

Ronald Knox once said much the same thing about certain popular Marian devotions. He said their mawkish representations left him cold. Shortly after his death his comments engendered condemnation from a group that promoted the restricted, Feeneyite interpretation to *extra ecclesiam nulla salus*, "no salvation outside the Church." The group seemed to say that it wasn't enough to be a formal member of the Church. One's salvation also depended on liking the artistic style epitomized by nineteenth-century Italian holy cards.

> Thus the reality of any spiritual statement must be tested by the intellect, not by the imagination. The intellect's word of rejection is "inconceivable." This means that the statement proffered to the intellect contains a contradiction within itself, so that no concept can be formed embodying the statement. A four-sided triangle, for instance, is in this sense inconceivable.

It is a contradiction in terms, because a triangle is a three-sided figure, and a four-sided three-sided figure cannot be conceived and cannot *be*. The less-instructed atheist will ask whether God can make a weight so heavy that he cannot lift it, in the happy belief that, whatever answer we give, we shall admit that there is something God cannot do. But the question literally is meaningless: a weight that an omnipotent Being cannot lift is as complete a contradiction in terms as a four-sided triangle. In either case the words are English but do not mean anything because they cancel each other out. There is no point in piling together a lot of words, regardless of their meaning, and then asking triumphantly "Can God make that?" God can do *anything*, but a contradiction in terms is not a thing at all. It is nothing. God himself could not make a four-sided triangle or a weight that Almighty power could not lift. They are inconceivable; they are nothing; and nothing—to give a slightly different emphasis to Scripture—is impossible to God.

Sheed's reference to the "less-instructed atheist" reminds me of times when I would visit a local Unitarian church to listen to guest speakers trying to explain away Christianity. The predominant note was smugness. They were so convinced that Christianity had nothing to say for itself that they needed to levy nothing against it other than a sneer. I recall one regular audience member, an immigrant from Germany, who spoke darkly about "priestcraft." Others, in dismissing arguments for Christianity, thought it sufficient to remark that they were members of Mensa. It always has been a wonder to me how self-styled rationalists have such difficulty wielding syllogisms.

Thus the first test of any statement concerning spiritual reality is not can imagination form a mental picture of it, but does it stand up to the examination of the intellect, do the terms of it contradict each other, is it conceivable or inconceivable? Imagination can say nothing about it either way. It cannot reject it. It cannot accept it either. It must leave it alone, and that is precisely one of the things that imagination hates to do.

Which leads us to the other of the two ways in which imagination hinders intellect without our perceiving it. In the ordinary way, if concepts are beyond its reach, imagination acts as censor and simply throws them out, while the intellect, grown flabby with disuse, tiredly concurs in a rejection so beneficent because it saves so much trouble. But this happy arrangement receives a check if one happens to be a Catholic. For the Faith binds us to accept many truths altogether beyond imagination's reach and will not allow imagination to reject them. Here imagination does its subtlest piece of sabotage. It cannot forbid intellect to accept them, so it offers to *help* intellect to accept them. It comes along with all sorts of mental pictures, comparisons from the material world. Thus for the doctrine of the Blessed Trinity imagination offers the picture of a shamrock, or a triangle, or three drops of water poured together to form one drop of water.

Now there is in fact a definite role for such analogies as these in religion. God's dealings with mankind may often be seen more clearly by some comparison drawn from the material universe, because both human beings and the material universe are creatures of the same God, and there are all kinds of family resemblances between the various works of the one master. Our Lord's parables are a marvelous application of this principle. But useful as such comparisons may be as illustrations of God's dealings with us, they shed no light whatever upon the innermost being of God in himself. The shamrock simile tells us absolutely nothing about the Blessed Trinity, nor does the triangle, or the drops of water. The excuse for them is that they help us to *see* the doctrine. But they do not. They only help us to swallow the doctrine. They prevent the doctrine from being a difficulty, but they do it by substituting something else for the doctrine, something which is not a difficulty, certainly, but not the doctrine either. What is the gain of this, I do not know.

Certainly it prevents the truth about God from being a danger to our faith, but, in the same act, it prevents the truth about God from being a light to our minds. The same objective might have been attained a great deal more neatly by not mentioning the doctrine at all.

Until I read Frank Sheed on the Trinity, I don't think I ever found an explanation that could be transferred usefully to an audience. It is one thing to read Aquinas or a precis of Aquinas and murmur to oneself, "Yes, that make perfect sense and explains the mystery as well as mortal man can explain it," but it is something else to find an explanation that can be presented to people disinclined to tackle a fat treatise on theology.

When I first read Sheed's claim that, of all the topics handled at open-air meetings, the Trinity was the one that consistently drew the largest and most interested crowds, I momentarily balked. The Trinity is the root doctrine of Christianity because it concerns the inner nature of God himself. Everything else is subsidiary to that; everything else flows from that. But since the doctrine of the Trinity is, in a way, the doctrine furthest from us, with all the distance that lies between a creature and his Creator, it strikes one at first as too ethereal to grasp and, frankly, a bit boring because abstract. Why should a crowd be drawn to this belief above all others? Its seeming novelty? When was the last time the crowd heard someone refer to the Trinity, except ritualistically, such as when making the sign of the cross? When the unchurched or lightly churched think of Christianity, they may think of moral teachings or Church leaders or historical embarrassments. It isn't the Trinity that first pops into mind. So what was the fascination?

The notion is unfortunately widespread that the mystery of the Blessed Trinity is a mystery of mathematics, that is to say, of how one can equal three. The plain Christian accepts the doctrine of the Trinity; the "advanced" Christian rejects it; but too often what is being accepted by the one and rejected by the other is that one equals three. The believer argues that God has

80

said it, therefore it must be true; the rejecter argues that it cannot be true, therefore God has not said it. A learned non-Catholic divine, being asked if he believed in the Trinity, answered, "I must confess that the arithmetical aspect of the Deity does not greatly interest me"; and if the learned can think that there is some question of arithmetic involved, the ordinary person hardly can be expected to know any better.

Consider what happens when a believer in the doctrine is suddenly called upon to explain it—and note that unless he is forced to, he will not talk about it at all. There is no likelihood of his being so much in love with the principal doctrine of the Faith that he will *want* to tell people about it. Anyhow, here he is: he has been challenged and must say something. The dialogue runs something like this:

Believer: "Well, you see, there are three persons in one nature."

Questioner: "Tell me more."

Believer: "Well, there is God the Father, God the Son, God the Holy Spirit."

Questioner: "Ah, I see, three gods."

Believer: "Oh, no! Only one God."

Questioner: "But you said three: you called the Father God, which is one; and you called the Son God, which makes two; and you called the Holy Spirit God, which makes three."

Here the dialogue breaks down. From the believer's mouth there emerges what can only be called a soup of words, sentences that begin and do not end, words that change into something else halfway. This goes on for a longer or shorter time. But finally there comes something like: "Thus, you see, three is one and one is three." The questioner naturally retorts that three is not one nor one three. Then comes the believer's great moment. With his eyes fairly gleaming he cries: "Ah, that is the mystery. You have to have faith."

"It's a mystery to me"—which means about the same as "It's Greek to me"—indicates that there is something we know nothing about. The sentence is a verbal shrug. That may be the colloquial use of *mystery*, but it is not the theological use. A mystery is not something about which we can know nothing. It is something about which we would not know anything had the fact of the mystery not been given to us through revelation. Once it has been given—once we have been told of its existence and of some of its attributes—we have information to go on. However much or little is revealed to us, our minds will set to work drawing out the implications.

There is the mystery of the Hypostatic Union: God incarnate, superadding human nature to his divine nature. In the early Church this rankled many because it seemed so implausible, even offensive to those who thought that God was "wholly other" in the most extreme way. The result was Arianism, which held that Christ had but one nature, the human, and Arianism's opponent, Monophysitism, which agreed that he had but one nature but that it was the divine. The dueling heresies were not true opposites; they arose from the same principle—that in Christ there could be only one nature. The only question was which one. Arians and Monophysites were united in their opposition to mystery—or at least to the revealed mystery of the Incarnation. The result was that Christ was the best of all creatures but not God (Arianism) or was God disguised as a creature (Monophysitism).

I don't recall ever meeting an Arian or a Monophysite—at least not anyone conscious of holding one of those positions in its classical form—but, like most Americans, I have had rejecters of divine mysteries come to my door: Jehovah's Witnesses, for example. They hold to a unitarian position, saying that in God there is only one person, not three. The faith of the Watchtower is a simplification of authentic Christianity, and simplification appeals to many people. It has some awkward consequences, though, if one tries to account for the whole of Scripture.

I recall lying on the sofa one summer Saturday. There was a knock at the door, and I got up to discover that two Jehovah's Witnesses were on the porch. I stepped outside to speak with them and learned that one woman was a former Methodist and the other a former Catholic. I told them that I was familiar with the history of the Watchtower, that I had read its magazines, and that I had a copy of *Reasoning from the Scriptures*, a book used to train its door-to-door missionaries.

Before the two women could commandeer the conversation, I suggested we read through John 6 in the Watchtower's New World translation. As we did so, I directed my remarks mainly to the former Catholic. I focused on Christ's Eucharistic discourse and its literalness, how he repeatedly said that we must eat his flesh and drink his blood, how those who took his words metaphorically turned away from him—first the Jews who were listening, then some of his own disciples who, until then, had accepted all that he had taught. I noted that in John 6 we find the only instance in Scripture in which anyone leaves Christ for a doctrinal reason.

Why that early opposition? Those who turned from him could not accept the mystery of the Eucharist. It made no sense to them; to some it seemed blasphemous. To all the naysayers it seemed impossible, and so it seemed to the Jehovah's Witnesses. Their church teaches that John 6 is a great example of symbolic teaching, but I said to the women that a fresh reading of the text shows that this wasn't so. Christ's listeners understood him to be speaking literally—because that is how he spoke. He was revealing what could not have been learned through human ratiocination alone: the mystery of the Real Presence.

It is no accident that those who reject one mystery tend to reject others. It is no surprise that the Jehovah's Witnesses reject not only the Trinity (and thus the Incarnation) but the Eucharist as well.

Now it is true that the doctrine of the Blessed Trinity is a mystery and that we can know it only by faith. But what we have just been hearing is not the mystery of the Trinity; it is not the mystery of anything. It is wretched nonsense. It may be heroic faith to believe like the man who "wished there were four of 'em that he might believe more of 'em" or it may be total intellectual unconcern—God has revealed things about himself, we accept the fact that he has done so but find in ourselves no particular inclination to follow it up. God has told us that he is three persons in one divine nature, and we say "Quite so," and proceed to think about other matters—last week's retreat or next week's confession or Lent or Lourdes or the Church's social teaching or foreign missions. . . .

How did we reach this curious travesty of the supreme truth about God? The short statement of the doctrine is, as we have heard all our lives, that there are three persons in one nature. But if we attach no meaning to the word *person*, and no meaning to the word *nature*, then both the nouns have dropped out of our definition, and we are left only with the numbers three and one and get along as best we can with these. . . .

We have seen that the imagination cannot help here. Comparisons drawn from the material universe are a hindrance and no help. Once one has taken hold of this doctrine, it is natural enough to want to utter it in simile and metaphor—like the lovely *lumen de lumine*, light of light, with which the Nicene Creed phrases the relation of the Son to the Father. But this is for afterward, poetical statement of the truth known, not the way to its knowledge. For that, the intellect must go on alone. And for the intellect, the way into the mystery lies, as we have already suggested, in the meaning of the words "person" and "nature." There is no question of arithmetic involved. We are not saying three persons in one person or three natures in one nature; we are saying three persons in one nature. There is not even the appearance of an arithmetical problem. It is for us to see what person is and what nature is and then to consider what meaning there can be in a nature totally possessed by three distinct persons. . . .

One distinction we see instantly. Nature answers the question *what* we are; person answers the question *who* we are. Every being has a nature; of every being we may properly ask, What is it? But not every being is a person: only rational beings are persons. We could not properly ask of a stone or a potato or an oyster, Who is it?

By our nature, then, we are what we are. It follows that by our nature we do what we do, for every being acts according to what it is. Applying this to ourselves, we come upon another distinction between person and nature. We find that there are many things, countless things, we can do. We can laugh and cry and walk and talk and sleep and think and love. All these and other things we can do because as human beings we have a nature that makes them possible. A snake could do only one of them—sleep. A stone could do none of them. Nature, then, is to be seen not only as what we are but as the source of what we can do.

But although my nature is the source of all my actions, although my nature decides what kind of operations are possible for me, it is not my nature that does them. I do them, I the person. Thus both person and nature may be considered sources of action, but in a different sense. The person is that which does the actions; the nature is that by which the actions are done or, better, that from which the actions are drawn. We can express the distinction in all sorts of ways. We can say that it is our *nature* to do certain things. We can say that *we* operate in or according to our *nature*. In this light we see why the philosophers speak of a person as the center of attribution in a rational nature: whatever is done in a rational nature or suffered in a rational nature or any way experienced in a rational nature is done or suffered or experienced by the person whose nature it is. . . .

With all the light we can get on the meaning of person and of nature even in ourselves, we have seen that there is still much that is dark to us. Both concepts plunge away to a depth where the eye cannot follow them. Even of our own finite natures, it would be rash to affirm that the only possible relation is one person to one nature. But of an infinite nature, we have no experience at all. If God tells us that his own infinite nature is totally possessed by three persons, we can have no grounds for doubting the statement, although we may find it almost immeasurably difficult to make any meaning of it. There is no difficulty in accepting it as true, given our own inexperience of what it is to have an infinite nature and God's statement on the subject; there is no difficulty, I say, in accepting it as true. The difficulty lies in seeing what it means. Yet short of seeing some meaning in it, there is no point in having it revealed to us; indeed, a revelation that is only darkness is a kind of contradiction in terms.

Summarizing thus far, we may state the doctrine in this way: the Father possesses the whole nature of God as his own, the Son possesses the whole nature of God as his own, the Holy Spirit possesses the whole nature of God as his own. Thus, since the nature of any being decides what the being is, each person is God, wholly and therefore equally with the others. Further, the nature decides what the person can do; therefore, each of the three persons who then totally possess the divine nature can do all the things that go with being God.

This extended excerpt shows well Sheed's skill as an apologist: clarity, precision, winsomeness. In his lengthy 1929 essay on Dante, T.S. Eliot said, "Dante and Shakespeare divide the modern world between them; there is no third." If I were to venture something similar about Catholic apologetics, at least in the English-speaking world, I would say that Sheed and Arnold Lunn divide the modern apologetics world between them. My favorite apologist in terms of wit and style is Ronald Knox, but he engaged in apologetics only sporadically. Sheed and Lunn devoted the greater part of their mid- and late-life creative energies to an energetic defense of the Faith. Their books are worth reading repeatedly. Whenever I take them down from the shelf and flip the pages, I come to penciled marks in the margins, my way of indicating something worth recapturing: a puissant argument, a memorable locution, a way of conveying Catholic truth that always seems fresh and compelling.

7

A Catholic Dictionary

Donald Attwater

My use of this fat book subverted the editor's intention.

In his preface Donald Attwater (1892–1977) explains that this book was conceived in 1928 "as a simple dictionary of the technical words and phrases of the Catholic Church." Even in the preparatory stages it grew beyond that and become more encyclopedic. It "became a general work of quick reference to the signification of the words, terms, names, and phrases in common use in the philosophy, dogmatic and moral theology, canon law, liturgy, institutions, and organization of the Catholic Church. It looks primarily at present-day belief, practice, teaching, opinion, or as the case may require, and therefore history, exposition, and apologetics are strictly secondary and subordinate, and biography has no place at all."

The last phrase is verified easily. The dictionary has entries for the "Rule of St. Augustine," "Augustinian Nuns," the "Augustinians of the Assumption," and "Augustinism" but no entry for the saint himself. There are entries for the "Leonine City," the "Leonine Sacramentary," and the "Leonine Union," but no pope named Leo gets an entry of his own. So it goes, no matter which character of Church history is searched for.

Attwater's insistence that the dictionary treated apologetics as "strictly secondary and subordinate" did not dissuade me from using his work as an apologetical tool. On every page I found something useful for my work. As I flip the pages now, I find a faded bookmark at the start of the letter S, and I see double vertical pencil marks beside the entry for "Sacraments, Non-Catholic"—marks I made perhaps three decades ago. This is a short entry but one that must have seemed particularly useful to me:

In the dissident Eastern and other non-Catholic churches which have valid episcopal orders those sacraments which of their nature require only valid orders, and not power of jurisdiction as well, are also valid. (The Church by her practice recognizes the validity also of penance and confirmation administered by an Orthodox priest.) They are also subjectively efficacious for sanctification and salvation, in accordance with Pope Clement XI's condemnation of the proposition that "outside the Church no grace is given." The "sacraments" of Christian bodies without valid orders, e.g., the Anglican, may be the occasions of the conferring of divine grace but cannot be the vehicle of that grace, having no objective validity, except those of baptism and matrimony.

My penciled highlight stood against the sentence that mentions Clement XI, but the whole entry was of use to me, not just in my dealings with Protestants but also with Catholics. The very concision of the entry forced me to keep several things in mind at once, and, as I read sentence by sentence, I was conscious of questions and difficulties that I had attempted to handle in the past and no doubt would be expected to handle in the future.

The entry can be divided into three. The first affirms that all of the churches of the East, if they have valid priestly orders, have valid sacraments. This, of course, I well knew, but I also well knew that many people I dealt with didn't know this. They presumed that the Russian Orthodox, for example, had no valid sacraments; this ignorance was as true of Catholics as of non-Catholics. A subsidiary point, as stated in the entry, is that the Catholic Church recognizes, at least for the Eastern Orthodox, that those churches also have valid penance and confirmation, the implication being that they also have valid jurisdiction, which is necessary for those two sacraments to "take."

Then comes the second part of the entry, which foreshadowed my future dealings with Catholics who, so insistent on the true principle that "outside the Church there is no salvation," argued that "outside the Church there is no grace." They found themselves backing into such a position because, in many cases, they sensed a problem: if valid baptism exists outside the Church (say, as administered by Protestants), then that baptism, being efficacious, must convey sanctifying grace, and someone dying in that grace would be saved. This looked to them as though it meant that *extra ecclesiam nulla salus* was not really true.

Their problem was not really a conflict between the proposition that grace abounds outside the Church and the principle that there is no salvation outside the Church, because the two statements are not in opposition, if properly understood, but they did not see that. It proved useful in discussion to bring up Clement XI's teaching. He was not a modern pope who could be suspected of underhandedly trying to reinterpret traditional doctrine. He reigned three centuries ago, never was regarded as an innovator, and is best remembered for issuing the bull *Unigenitus*, which condemned Jansenism. (I admit that, for some proponents of the strictest interpretation of *extra ecclesiam nulla salus*, my use of Clement's name was ineffective: they were predisposed to dislike him since they had Jansenistic tendencies of their own.)

The third part of the dictionary entry stated two important things, one to confound Protestants and the other to confound, again, certain Catholics. With concision the entry notes that "the 'sacraments' of Christian bodies without valid orders"—this includes all Protestant churches, including the Anglican—have "no objective validity." These bodies generally do not say "sacraments" but instead say "ordinances" or similar terms. Whichever the descriptor, these religious rites convey no grace on their own, yet these rites can "be the occasions of the conferring of divine grace." How can that be?

Whatever grace is conferred comes through the intentionality of the recipients of these acts. Consider the "Lord's Supper," as practiced in various denominations. No transubstantiation occurs; in fact, the very idea of transubstantiation is repugnant to most of these bodies. But participants in the "Lord's Supper" participate in what they understand to be an act of worship;

they *will* to worship in emulation of the Lord's Supper that is recorded in the New Testament, and it is that willing that brings to them graces, even though those are not, properly speaking, sacramental graces, because no true sacrament is occurring.

I say that this third part of the entry confounds both Protestants and Catholics. The first are confounded because their rituals, even when called "sacraments," are not in fact sacraments and cannot, in themselves, transmit grace. Some Catholics are confounded because they wish to maintain the position that within Protestantism no grace can be found at all. This is not, of course, a position held by many Catholics, but over the years I have had to deal with it more often than one might expect.

As a final point, this dictionary entry notes that baptism and matrimony are exceptions to what has been said. Even in Christian bodies that have no valid priestly orders and thus no valid equivalent of the Eucharist or most other sacraments, baptism and matrimony can be administered validly. The reason is that neither sacrament requires priestly participation. In the other sacraments, it is the priest (or bishop, who holds the plenitude of priesthood) who confects the sacraments—this is most evident in the Eucharist: no priest, no Mass. But baptism and matrimony can be conferred by lay people. In the case of matrimony, the bride and groom confer the sacrament on themselves through their exchange of vows. A priest serves as a witness, in the normal course of things, but a true marriage would result in the stereotypic stranded-on-a-desert-island scenario where the man and woman find themselves forced to live on their own. As for baptism, it can be conferred by anyone, even a non-Christian, so long as the person performing the baptism recites the right words ("I baptize you in the name of the Father, and of the Son, and of the Holy Spirit") while administering water. The only requirement is that the baptizer will to do whatever the Catholic Church wills to do in baptism, even if he does not understand what the Church wills.

Such, anyway, were observations that came to me in first reading this short entry in *A Catholic Dictionary*. The entry served as an organizer of my thoughts and a reminder of what I would need to cover when trying to address the topic of "non-Catholic sacraments." I do not recall whether I read Attwater's book straight through. I suspect not, though over time I may have read all of it, bouncing around as I once bounced around in the James and James *Mathematical Dictionary*.

8

A Dictionary of the Popes

Donald Attwater

Sometimes we remember quotations wrongly but in words better than the original.

My favorite misremembered papal quotation comes from Leo XIII's 1891 encyclical *Rerum Novarum*. This is how it settled in my mind: "There is nothing so salutary as to view the world as it really is." (A corollary might be: "There is nothing so salutary as to view ourselves as we really are.") This is something every apologist should keep in mind. Ours is a religion extended through history and manifested through imperfect members, most of whom have had more faults than virtues, as we can demonstrate sufficiently by looking in a mirror. The first line of defense of the Church is to acknowledge what the Church is and has been—in fact, not in idealization. "You are to be perfect, as your heavenly Father is perfect" was not an existential description.

In a letter written in 1889 to Cardinal Jean-Baptiste-Francois Pitra, who collaborated in the production of *Patrologia Latina* and *Patrologia Graeca*, Leo wrote, "The historian of the Church has a duty not to dissimulate any of the trials that the Church has had to suffer from the faults of her children and even at times from those of her own ministers." Here the pope echoed his distant predecessor, Leo the Great: "The dignity of Peter is not diminished even by an unworthy successor."

These were points kept in mind as Donald Attwater wrote *A Dictionary of the Popes*, which appeared a few months after Pius XII assumed the Chair of Peter in 1939. "The object of this book is to provide in handy form a record of the principal events of the life of each of the popes," begins Attwater. "[I]t does not aim at being a one-volume history of the papacy as an institution, much less such a history of the Universal Church, and therefore I have, in the main, confined myself to those matters in which the pope took an official or personal part." Attwater said that he relied on "the guidance of two great Catholic scholars": Horace K. Mann, who wrote the *Lives of the Popes in the Early Middle Ages* (eighteen volumes), and Ludwig von Pastor, who wrote *The History of the Popes* (twenty-nine volumes).

In reading this dictionary I discovered many little things that proved useful in later years and one big thing. The big thing was confirmation of what I already knew: the Church has been blessed with an extraordinary wealth of holy and intelligent popes (particularly the former), plus a few men who never should have been popes at all (or ordained at all). The best of the popes made less-than-ideal decisions; the worst of them failed to injure the Church permanently. By all human measures, the papacy should have collapsed centuries ago, either during the centuries of persecution or during the centuries when so many popes thought of themselves as kings first and priests second.

As I said, those were things I already appreciated, but I discovered confirmation of them in Attwater's book. I also discover little things that came in handy when in disputes or discussions—not just with non-Catholics but also with Catholics. I learned, for example, that Victor I, whose decade-long reign ended in 199, was "the first bishop of Rome to celebrate the Holy Mysteries in Latin instead of Greek." That nugget helped me put liturgical development into perspective when speaking to fellow Latin-Mass attendees who uncritically accept the notion that the Latin Mass is "the Mass of all ages"; for most ages, perhaps, but not for all.

In 2000 I attended the wedding of my niece in Tokyo. Like most Japanese, she is not a Christian. The ceremony was held in the wedding chapel of a major hotel. In Japan, the saying goes, you are married Shinto and buried Buddhist, so this was a Shinto ceremony. Only the immediate families were present. We sat facing one another in what looked like the choir stalls of a European church, the bride's family on the left side, the groom's on the right. The bridal couple sat and stood, as the situation required, in the center, facing the Shinto priest and his assistants.

I understood hardly a word of the ceremony, since it was conducted in archaic Japanese, but I understood something Chesterton once had written. He said that non-believers commonly say that all religions teach the same but that their ministers dress differently. Chesterton insisted the opposite was true: all religions teach differently but their ministers dress the same. He may not have had Shinto beliefs and Shinto priests in mind when he said that, but I saw that he was right.

The priest officiating at the wedding wore vestments, including analogues of a Catholic priest's stole, surplice, and chasuble. Of course the cut for each was different from the Catholic form, but the Shinto "chasuble" was recognizable as such and perhaps had a similar origin to the Catholic, which developed from a standard Roman overcoat.

It was the first pope named Stephen who issued the first regulations on priestly attire. The *Liber Pontificalis* reports, notes Attwater, that "he ordered that clothes worn by clerics at church services were to be kept for that purpose and not taken into daily use or worn by laymen." Over time fashions would change, not just for laymen but also for clerics in their workaday capacities, but Stephen's order seems to have been the first step in ossifying liturgical attire. I found this point useful when dealing with Evangelicals and Fundamentalists who turned up their noses at vestments, used to seeing, as they were, their own ministers in modern business dress.

Of particular delight for me was learning about John II. He was the first pope who, on his election, dropped his given name and took a new name. In his case, it seemed particularly prudent, since his given name was Mercury. He seems to have thought it inappropriate for the vicar of Christ to bear the name of a pagan god.

John died in 535. Two lifetimes later, in 655, Martin I died. He was the last pope to die a martyr, but he hardly was the last pope to be abused. Pius VI and Pius VII both had much to suffer at Napoleon's hands, and popes before and after them have had their reputations besmirched by enemies of the Church, Pius XII being a prominent example.

Not so much recently, but in my earlier work as an apologist I found myself defending particular popes and the papacy in general from scurrilous attacks. The attacks came in all sorts. Some concerned papal morals, some concerned papal lineage, and some concerned papal wealth. I made no attempt to excuse the inexcusable, but I tried to show that the intellectual or moral failings of fallible men did not undermine the bona fides of an infallible Church. (Catholics hold that, in certain circumstances, popes are infallible. We never have held any of them to be impeccable.)

Of course, there was the charge—seemingly universal among Fundamentalists—that the "number of the beast" was a code for the pope. But which pope? No particular one, apparently. Some accusers said the number referred to the papacy as a whole. Not a few times I had public exchanges with anti-Catholics who, in a display of erudition, noted that when traditional numerical values were given to the letters of one of the titles of the popes, *Vicarius Filii Dei*, the sum was 666. I willingly conceded their arithmetic but as willingly noted that *Vicarius Filii Dei* (Vicar of the Son of God) never had been a papal title. The authentic title was, and remains, *Vicarius Christi* (Vicar of Christ), which— unfortunately for the anti-Catholics—does not sum to 666. If my opponents were Seventh-day Adventists, I happily showed them that the name of the founder of their sect, Ellen Gould White, actually does tally to 666.

9

Fundamentals of Catholic Dogma

Ludwig Ott

This is the theological analogue of the James and James *Mathematical Dictionary*, which I mention in the preface. No one reads any dictionary straight through, other than publishers' proofreaders. When I was young, I dipped into James and James to refresh myself on mathematical techniques that already were fading from my memory and to learn new techniques that might stand me well at math tournaments. Similarly with Ott. No one with a social life would read this book straight through. There is no plot, in the normal sense, although there is a Hero. This is a densely-packed compendium of all Catholic teachings, divided into five constituent books: God as Unity and Trinity, God as Creator, God as Redeemer, God as Sanctifier, and God as Consummator (that is, eschatology).

Ludwig Ott (1906–1985) was a German theologian ordained in 1930. His specialty was dogmatics, and this book became a standard manual in ten languages. The editor of the English edition, James Bastible, dean of Cork Cathedral, calls it "quite the most remarkable work of compression of its kind that I have encountered." I would have to agree with that. Each time I open Ott's book I marvel at how much he packs on a page. It would be improper to call his work an outline; that would give the wrong impression. It is filled with nested divisions, but "outline" leads one to think that each sub-point consists of just a few words. Not so. Some sub-points go on for several dense paragraphs, with many references and quotations from obscure sources. I imagine the author must have been a man who seldom left his home, spending his days and evenings sitting in an overstuffed chair beneath a lamp's glare, steadily working his way through his massive private library. He must have developed an efficient system for annotating and cross-referencing the hundreds of texts he studied so that, when the time came for it, he could gather together all pertinent material on some focused topic—and this in the days before computerized databases.

In the foreword to the second edition, Bastible says, "As the author mentions in his preface, the object is to provide a basic course." Well. That is much like Thomas Aquinas saying that his *Summa Theologiae* was intended for beginners—which it was, and so with Ott's book, though it hardly is likely that any work as rigorous as this will be found today in any theological curriculum for beginners, and I wonder whether more advanced students are presented with anything so detailed and ordered. (Mindful of lessened academic standards, Bastible remarks that "all Latin quotations have been translated wherever this seemed necessary to enable a reader, whose Latin is rusty, to follow the text with ease." Note the exquisite courtesy of "whose Latin is rusty.")

From the title, one might think that *Fundamentals of Catholic Dogma* is little more than an extended listing of Catholic beliefs. It certainly is that, but it is much more than that. I found its chief utility not in fleshing out the creeds but in the patristic and historical explanations that are given. It is one thing to know that Christ has two natures. It is something else to know about ancient heresies relating to those natures, such as Arianism and Monophysitism, and to have those heresies put into historical perspective. Connections then can be made to our own time, when those heresies have been revived but under new names and, in the cases of most holders, with no knowledge that what is new to them is very old indeed.

The introduction to *Fundamentals of Catholic Dogma* is especially useful for the budding apologist who is trying to situate the corpus of Catholic teaching in his mind. Ott begins by distinguishing natural theology, as expounded by ancient philosophers such as Plato, and supernatural theology, which is natural theology under divine revelation. Natural theology was enough to prove God's existence, and many of his attributes, through reason alone, but reason had its limits. Only with revelation could man obtain an adequate (though still highly circumscribed) understanding of reality.

Some modern Christians think that whatever is known about God is known through faith. Perhaps they have a suspicion regarding the role of reason; perhaps they have no experience with the ancient Greeks and Romans. If belief in God's existence were a matter of faith and not of reason, no atheist could be faulted for his disbelief, since faith, as Christians will attest, is a free gift, offered to some and not to others. One who is not offered a gift is not faulted for not having been offered it. Ott demonstrates sufficiently what the Church always has taught: that God's existence and many of his attributes can be known through reason. Later, the result of reasoning is supplemented with revelation; faith has a part of play at this stage, but reason is not set aside, since what is revealed is itself reasonable.

Of particular interest to me, since I like classifications, is Ott's section on the classification of dogmas and the following section on the development of dogma. All of his references are ancient. I was a little disappointed to see no citation from John Henry Newman's *Essay on the Development of Christian Doctrine*, but then Newman was an Englishman and Ott a German, and that may be explanation enough. (As perhaps a counter-balance, Ott frequently cites Luther as the best bad example of certain theological opinions: one German versus another.)

As with James and James, so with Ott: from him I learned much that was interesting but useless in practice. In a section on "The Trinitarian Perichoresis (Circumincession)"—that is, how the three divine Persons are "in" one another—he refers to two terms that differ only in one internal letter: circumincession versus circuminsession. "The word *circumincessio* expresses more the idea of the active penetration, the latter *circuminsessio* more the idea of the passive coinherence [of one divine Person with respect to another]. The former corresponds more to the Greek, the latter more to the Latin way of looking at it."

I never have found an opportunity to speak publicly about circumincession over against circuminsession. Perhaps I never will. Unless I find myself asked to speak about the subtleties that distinguish the thinking of the Christian West from that of the Christian East, this will remain a theological nicety that I never will be able to put into play. Pity.

Throughout his book Ott brings clarity to easily misunderstood issues. Take original sin as an example. He says, "Original sin does not consist, as the Reformers, the Baians, and the Jansenists taught, in 'the habitual concupiscence which remains, even in the baptized, a true and proper sin but is no longer reckoned for punishment.'" This is a common misunderstanding with today's Protestants, particularly those of a Calvinistic bent. Ott continues: "The Council of Trent teaches that through baptism everything is taken away which is a true and proper sin and that the concupiscence which remains behind after baptism for the moral proving is called sin in an improper sense only. That sin remains in man, even if it is not reckoned for punishment, is irreconcilable with the Pauline teaching of justification as an inner transformation and renewal." We're stuck with concupiscence, but concupiscence itself is not sin, though it is an evil that tends us toward sin.

It is fine distinctions such as these that make Ott an especially useful instructor for the apologist.

Is Christianity True?

Arnold Lunn and C.E.M. Joad

DELIGHT IN GENTLEMANLY CONTROVERSY

This collection of thirty-eight letters between Arnold Lunn (1888–1974) and C.E.M. Joad (1891–1953) was written between March and November 1932 and occupied 378 pages in book format. Joad, then an agnostic and later an Anglican, taught philosophy at the University of London's Birkbeck College. Lunn was not yet a Catholic and was known best for his works on mountaineering and for his early *roman à clef, The Harrovians.* (He had attended Harrow.)

Lunn entered the Catholic Church in July 1933, eight months after his last letter to Joad and twenty-two months after his last letter to Ronald Knox in an exchange that appeared as *Difficulties.* Lunn later wrote, "I can imagine no better training for the Church than to spend, as I did, a year arguing the case against Catholicism with a Catholic, and a second year in defending the Catholic position against an agnostic."

Joad and Lunn had met at the former's home, and Lunn begins with a disclosure: he is in the midst of a similar book with yet another writer.

> I accept your challenge to discuss Christianity in a series of letters in spite of the fact that I am supposed to be engaged in a book, somewhat similar in scope, with J.B.S. Haldane. Haldane, however, has written only

one letter in the last six months, and I am beginning to suspect that he will appear before his Maker before I have succeeded in convincing him that his Maker exists. I have written to him to say that I am accepting your challenge on the understanding that we confine ourselves to Christianity in particular, rather than to the alleged conflict between science and supernaturalism which is to be the theme of my letters with Haldane if those letters are ever written.

Lunn's exchange with Haldane eventually appeared as *Science and the Supernatural*. Now back to his letters to Joad.

I suggest that you and I should divide our correspondence into two parts, in the first of which you might perhaps explain why you are not a Christian, and in the second of which I shall explain why I am.

I accept your challenge with great pleasure.

In the first place, though we differ on fundamental issues, we are not personally antipathetic. When we first discussed this book you said that you would never agree to exchange controversial letters over a period of months with a man whom you disliked. Nor should I, and I feel that the ritualistic handshake which we shall exchange before we start hammering away at each other is not purely formal. We have certain tastes in common; the reproductions of Italian and Dutch primitives which hang around your library reassured me when I first called on you. There is always hope for a man, however perverse his views, who prefers Van Eyck to the post-impressionists.

This paragraph has stuck with me through the years. I delight in its delight of gentlemanly controversy, which can occur only between two men who treat one another gentlemanly. Unfortunately for Lunn, he was not able to begin his last book of correspondence with a similar paragraph. That book, published in 1946, was *Is the Church Anti-Social?*

Lunn's opponent was medieval historian G.G. Coulton (1858–1947). The two men did not get along. Coulton was an inveterate anti-Catholic and often found himself at odds, during the 1930s, with Hilaire Belloc, who in their exchanges gave him little quarter. Lunn was a milder opponent (nearly everyone was a milder opponent, when compared to Belloc), but his mildness did not preserve him from frustration. He and Coulton had agreed to a word count for their book (which is much shorter than the Lunn-Joad exchange). Coulton used up nearly all of his allotment in his first letter, thereby throwing off the book's balance. He was more interested in making a blast against the Church than in cooperating to produce a book that had the syncopation that readers expected from an exchange of letters. *Is the Church Anti-Social?* turned out to be Coulton's last book—he died the year after its publication—and the last such exchange that Lunn engaged in.

I long have wanted to participate in one of these exchanges of letters, though today such a book would be cobbled together from emails. I nearly had one arranged with John H. Armstrong, an Evangelical author engaged in ecumenical work. I developed an outline of how a book might be constructed, and he approved the format. The sticking point was a topic. Armstrong's interests at the time were mainly about the Eucharist. He had come to a belief similar, he said, to the Eastern Orthodox understanding. That meant we differed somewhat on the topic, but we didn't differ enough to produce a book of controversy—or at least not one that could be extended beyond a few pages. The project was shelved. I still hope to find an appropriate opponent—perhaps someone who appreciates Van Eyck. The problem is the gentlemanliness factor. There would be no problem locating an opponent who thinks an argument should be conducted chiefly with a cudgel; I can think of several Protestant controversialists who would jump at an opportunity to go at it with a Catholic, but the names that come to mind are of men who would be my Coultons and not my Joads. Coming up with a suitable topic seems to be easier than coming up with a suitable opponent.

> Secondly, you are a good controversialist, with whom it will be a pleasure to cross swords. I admired your handling

of Mr. [Morris Raphael] Cohen [1880–1947] in your debate with that sturdy survivor of Victorian materialism. And you are not only an expert, but also a good-tempered controversialist. You give and take hard blows, as I have good reason to know, with imperturbable good humour. It should be as easy for a controversialist to keep his temper when the argument runs against him as for a chess player to avoid hurtling the board on to the floor when mate is threatened, and good-humoured controversialists are rare. Nothing is more cramping to controversy than a sensitive opponent who construes as personal a purely impersonal attack on the arguments which he has advanced. It is a relief to feel that you and I prefer to dispense with the buttons on our foils.

Notice Lunn's appreciation of Joad's good temper. It is a pity that so little of today's controversial exchanges aren't done good-naturedly. This is most obvious in partisan politics, but it is true in religion also, as a few hours online will attest. Insults are more common than insights. This is as true among Catholics as among Protestants or non-believers.

In the third place, I welcome this correspondence because I admire your philosophical writings, which are lucid and well expressed.

In the fourth place, I welcome this correspondence because I do not in the least admire your religious writings, which are confused, badly expressed, and plagiaristic. There is evidence of hard thinking in every line that you write on philosophy, but you give your brain a rest when you turn to the uncongenial subject of Christianity. You may console yourself, however, with the reflection that in this respect you are not unique. In your attitude towards Christianity, you are a child of your age, an age which has decided that all standards of sober criticism may be suspended when Christianity is in the dock. H.G. Wells, [Julian] Huxley, and many another modern prophets display in their attitude to the greatest of all problems the same distressing blend of glib assurance and ignorance. In due course I must try to diagnose the malady, but first I must convince you that you yourself are suffering from this modern complaint.

Two things struck me when reading these last two paragraphs. First was Lunn's cheekiness: "I admire your philosophical writing," but "I do not in the least admire your religious writings." He was blunt in a good way. He was willing to do more than concede that his opponent had good arguments, at least in certain fields. He felt no need to demonize anyone, but he felt a keen need for clarity: "Here you are right. There you are wrong. And you deserve better of yourself."

In his penultimate sentence Lunn mentions H.G. Wells, known today mainly for his science-fiction novels, such as *The Time Machine* and *The War of the Worlds*. Like Coulton, Wells had found a Catholic opponent in Hilaire Belloc, who had written a book criticizing the anti-Catholic attitude of Wells's most influential work, *An Outline of History*, which was published in 1920 and sold widely. Wells replied with a book of his own, and Belloc wrote yet another book in reply. It was obvious that the two men had scant respect for one another. Wells had even less respect for the Catholic Church.

During World War II, Wells served as the British government's minister of Allied propaganda. Not long after retiring from that position, the elderly Wells—he was seventy-six at the time—wrote *Crux Ansata*, a short and vitriolic attack on Catholicism. The flavor of the 1944 book is given by the title of its first chapter: "Why Do We Not Bomb Rome?" He did not mean that the Allies should bomb Mussolini's government (though he surely thought they should). He meant Rome as epitomized by the Vatican. Wells wanted the Church to be bombed out of existence. He thought the war was an opportune time to eliminate Catholicism once and for all, beginning with the elimination of the papacy, then occupied by Pius XII. "Even in comparison with Fascism and the Nazi adventure, Roman Catholicism is a broken and utterly desperate thing, capable only of malignant mischief in our awakening world." Catholicism needed to be done away with, root and branch, and the Allies had the power to do it, thought Wells. He seemed disappointed that they didn't try. The year after the war ended, Wells died.

> My complaint against you, Mr. Wells, and Professor Julian Huxley is that you are all so unscientific in your attitude toward Christianity. It is unscientific to criticise a document without reading it; it is unscientific to bludgeon your opponent with unsupported assertions and unsubstantiated charges. All of you repeat, like a lesson learnt by rote at your mother's knee, the old, stale, stupid charge that the dogmas of the Church are at variance with science. None of you has ever deigned to give chapter and verse to this accusation. The Roman Catholic Church is usually represented as the most hostile to science of all churches, and the most reactionary. I therefore offer you these alternatives. Either name a doctrine, *de fide* for Roman Catholics, which is at variance with the proven results of scientific research, or admit that you have made charges that you cannot substantiate.

Elsewhere Lunn wrote that for years writers had been complaining about the Church's supposed opposition to science and its brutalization of scientists, but all the arguments reduced to one case: Galileo. Remove Galileo from consideration, and it was like a fire being deprived of all oxygen. But even with Galileo there was no case. If the Church really had been an opponent of science—and not, arguably, its progenitor, in proto-scientists such as Albert the Great—one would expect to find innumerable Galileo-like cases, but they never materialized, and even the Galileo case, if studied well, hardly can be construed as an attack upon science itself.

The problem with the Galileo case was Galileo, a headstrong man if a fairly devout Catholic. He arrogated to himself the interpretation of Scripture. Had he stuck to science and not intruded onto exegesis, there would have been no case, just as there had been no case against Copernicus, who earlier advanced the heliocentric theory. As for Galileo's punishment, he was subjected to house arrest, not a prison cell, and he lived a comfortable life, with visitors freely coming and going. This is not to justify the decision against him; undoubtedly the tribunal conducted the case poorly and Galileo was penalized more than he ought to have been. But his case, such as it is, is the chief evidence opponents of the Church bring up when asserting that the Church has been opposed to scientific inquiry, and it is weak evidence indeed.

What more interests me as an apologist is not so much the Galileo case itself, with its bureaucratic twists and turns, but the use made of the case in subsequent centuries, to the point that it became a talisman. There has been no need, in the minds of many, to argue the facts. It has been enough simply to proclaim "Galileo!", which commonly puts an end to discussion before it can start. The Galileo case, as a potent symbol, is just that—a symbol. Many people are satisfied to speak and think in terms of symbols, which is to say slogans. "Man lives not by bread alone but chiefly by catchwords," remarked Robert Louis Stevenson. So much of the case against the Church fails to rise above the level of catchwords. Many times I have listened to such complaints and felt the urge to say, "Here, let me make the argument against the Church. I can do a better job than you can." And I can, knowing the Church from within and knowing that all legitimate complaints against the Church reduce to complaints against its members, not against it teachings.

> When I read the modern prophets I am impressed by their habit of passing on undocumented sneers and unsubstantiated criticism. There is a painful lack of originality about their attacks on Christianity. In your philosophical work you are at great pains to think out things for yourself, and your work is, in consequence, interesting and original. But any stick is good enough for Christianity. The same feeble, brittle twig is passed along from hand to hand in order to save yourselves the trouble of cutting another decaying branch from the decaying tree. . . .

It has just occurred to me that one or two of my remarks might be construed as aggressive, and this would be a pity, for it is precisely because I respect the high quality of your best work that I am forced, more in sorrow than in anger, to complain bitterly of your attitude to Christianity. When we first met—before the possibility of this correspondence had been broached—I suggested that we might arrange a public debate on the evidence for the Resurrection, and you replied that you had not enough time "to mug up the evidence." Now the Resurrection, if it occurred, was the most important event in the history of our planet, and while it seems strange to me that a distinguished professor such as yourself should never have found time "to mug up the evidence" for or against the Resurrection, it seems even stranger that you should have devoted so much of your time, in the press and elsewhere, to condemning Christianity, whose credentials you have never examined.

A distinguished Jesuit once remarked to me that he would approach the study of Buddhism, or indeed of any other religion, with vastly more reverence than your moderns vouch to Christianity. Life is clearly too short to examine the case for every creed, but there is something to be said for making a rule never to refer with contempt to any religion unless one has made an effort to investigate its claims. I happen, for instance, to regard Calvinism with contempt, but I refrained from expressing any opinion on this subject until I had taken the trouble to read Calvin's *Institutes*. And if even Calvinism should not be condemned unheard, surely the great religion of which Calvinism is an evil perversion deserves a more courteous hearing than it receives from our modern prophets. Here is a religion which has transformed the face of Europe and revolutionised the fabric of society, a religion which has profoundly affected every aspect of human activity from law to architecture. Surely it should be regarded as an integral part of a liberal education to master, at least in outline, the philosophy, history, and ethics of a religion which was accepted for centuries without question by the civilised world. It is a sin against culture to ignore Christianity, and it is an offense against good breeding to adopt an attitude of contemptuous superiority towards any creed which still commands the adherence of men of undisputed intellectual attainments.

I confess that, unlike Lunn, I have not read Calvin's *Institutes*. Whenever I tried, I found myself drawn away from it to some more evocative piece of writing, such as the phone book. At least I have taken a cue from Lunn. I have not had much to say about Calvinism, other than that I disagree with it wherever it disagrees with Catholicism. I would not attempt a full-throated refutation of it without first studying the chief work of its inventor. Since there are so many fields, even within religion, in which I have not done research, I have found myself often declining to give an opinion. That may have disappointed people who expected a Catholic apologist to operate as an oracle, able to offer up instant judgments on any religious topic, but it seemed the only proper thing to do. Not everyone can be omnicompetent, but it is no difficult thing to refrain from advertising one's incompetence.

And perhaps in your heart of hearts you will agree that a man writes himself down as a hopeless Philistine if he speaks with ignorant contempt of the faith which produced St. Francis, which inspired Dante, and which found expression in the canvases of Bellini and in the stones of Venice. Even if I believed Christianity to be a myth, I should still salute with melancholy respect the superstition which had inspired such supreme artists in song, in paint, and in stone and should still find it difficult to understand how a mere superstition could take form in so notable a synthesis of spiritual and secular beauty. In the course of this correspondence we shall no doubt hear a great deal about the crimes of Christianity. I will not try to anticipate your attack, but I suggest that you cannot in common decency damn Christianity for the Inquisition without thanking Christianity for Chartres.

This paragraph says a lot about Arnold Lunn. In all of his books he displayed a generosity of spirit, even before he became a Catholic, even before he became an overt proponent of Christianity. He never seemed to have been the "hopeless Philistine" whom he complains about here. He always had a lively appreciation for the historic role of the Church, and he expected his interlocutors to have a similar appreciation—and he didn't hesitate to point out when they didn't. Here Lunn notes, without quite saying so, that the argument for the Church not only is at the level of theological or historical logic but at the level of beauty, "in song, in paint, and in stone." If he were writing this a few decades later—he died in 1974—perhaps he would have appended "in liturgy," as a tribute to what the Mass had been in terms of beauty, compared to what it had become in his last years.

> Your second line of defence is that it is impossible to take Christianity seriously because Christianity is not one body of doctrine but "a complex of heterogeneous and frequently contradictory beliefs and practices." I have some sympathy for this complaint, for the Modernists have queered the pitch by allocating to themselves the title of "Christian" to which they have no claim.
>
> Your letter shows up the fatuity of attempting to attract the modern mind by sacrificing the supernatural. Our Modernists are so busy trying to reconcile Christianity with the latest fad and fashion that they do not pause to note the contemptuous rejection of their compromise, which is all the thanks they deserve and receive from moderns like you. I am confident that you yourself have far more sympathy with the pope than with Bishop Barnes.

This was Ernest Barnes (1874–1953), the Anglican bishop of Birmingham who, earlier in life, had been a mathematician. He was the most liberal bishop in the Church of England for many years, writing in 1947 a book that attacked the Virgin Birth and

Christ's resurrection. He was so well-known, and so complained about by orthodox believers, that he commonly was referred to solely by his surname.

> The more extreme forms of Modernism, which deny the supernatural and the Resurrection, attract more attention than they should, thanks to the publicity given to Modernism by the press. The press are deceived by the name; they tend to assume that Modernism means Christianity up-to-date. They have yet to discover that the only really modern movement in our religion is the return to dogma and the supernatural. It is only in comparatively recent times that a man who described himself as a Christian would dare to deny the godhead of Christ or the Resurrection.
>
> The essence of Christianity is not, as you suggest, certain geological or astronomical theories but the belief that Jesus Christ is God and that Jesus Christ rose from the dead. It is those beliefs which I propose to defend in these letters. I do not agree that the main beliefs of the different churches are contradictory. The medieval Catholic and modern revivalists, such as the Salvation Army, agree so far as the central doctrines of Christianity are concerned. And as for John XXIII and St. Francis, the former was a bad Catholic and the latter was a good Catholic, but the sinner and the saint both agreed in whole-heartedly accepting the Catholic faith.

A modern reader might be confused here. This John XXIII was not the pope who convened Vatican II but an anti-pope whose "papacy" lasted from 1410 to 1415. He was one of three claimants to the See of Peter in what became known as the Western Schism. In 1932, when Lunn was writing, Angelo Roncalli, the future (legitimate) pope, was serving as apostolic visitor in Bulgaria.

> I am left unmoved by your discovery that Christians differ, have differed, and will continue to differ on points of biblical exegesis. Very few of these differences are

modern, though you appear to suppose that Christians continued to accept with untroubled faith the literal accuracy of the Bible until the Victorian scientists opened their attack, whereupon, you would have us believe, panic broke out in the ranks of the Church. Bishops rushed to their Bibles to discover whether they could reconcile geology with Genesis, and, on discovering that they could not, began to jettison one doctrine of the Christian faith after another. The fact is, of course, that from the earliest days it was recognised that the Bible consisted mainly of history but also partly of poetry, and the question of whether certain difficult passages should be interpreted as history or poetry has been debated among Christians from the earliest times.

If you really suppose that Christianity is disproved because we are told that Christ descended into hell, modern science having proved that hell is not in the centre of the Earth, I can only refer you once again to St. Thomas's remark on the use of metaphor and allegory in the Bible.

You ask me what common authority is recognised by Christians, and you add: "To this question, I was in my innocence about to suggest the Bible." There may be Christians, such as the American Fundamentalists, who believe in the literal accuracy of the Bible and who make no attempt to justify this belief by reason, but we are, I take it, in this correspondence discussing the reasoned grounds on which intelligent people accept Christianity, not the emotional reactions of pious "will-to-believers." Obviously if I replied that I believed everything in the Bible, and that I believed by faith that the Bible was infallible, there would be no point in continuing this correspondence.

Here I wish Lunn had gone on a bit further and had been more explicit. He knew the distinction between inerrancy and infallibility. The Bible is inerrant but not infallible. It is not infallible because only an active agent can be infallible—or fallible. To be infallible is to be unable, under certain circumstances, to make a wrong decision, but a decision can be made only by an active agent, such as a human being or an angel. No book can make a decision, not even Holy Writ, and so it is improper to use either *fallible* or *infallible* with respect to the Bible. The proper word is *inerrant*, meaning that the Bible, when properly construed, contains no error in its teaching.

I am afraid that this letter will be terribly long, but it is largely your fault. It is impossible to argue about Christianity with a man who misconceives the basis of Christian apologetics. It is essential to clear the ground by removing this misconception, and you must therefore forgive me for outlining the classic argument on what the Christian relies.

Whether Christianity is reasonable is, I agree, a matter of opinion, but whether the Christian theologian appeals to reason is a question of fact. The argument may be summarised as follows: The existence of God, as I hope to show in a later letter, can be proved by pure reason. Natural theology is the science of deducing by reason those attributes of God which can be proved without recourse to revelation. Other facts about God, such as the doctrine of the Trinity, cannot be proved by reason and depend on revelation. Our next task must be therefore to discover whether God has revealed himself to man and to attempt to test, once again by pure reason, the credentials of any alleged revelation.

We now approach the Bible and approach it in the same spirit as that in which we should approach any other human document. We do not believe in the Bible merely because it is the Bible but because we are convinced of its veracity by rational inferences similar in kind to those which convince us of other historical facts. We do not, for instance, accept that Christ rose from the dead merely because we find the Resurrection recorded in the Gospels; we accept the Resurrection because, of all the theories which have been put forward to explain the origin of Christianity, the only theory which fits all the facts is the theory that Jesus of Nazareth claimed to be God and proved his claim by rising from the dead.

Thus far Catholics and Protestants are in agreement; they do not appeal either to faith, or to humility, or to authority, or to an infallible Bible in their attempt to prove the central doctrine of Christianity.

The Roman Catholic, then, claims to prove from the Bible, which he is still treating as a purely human document, that Christ intended to found an infallible Church. Where, then, is this Church? The Roman Catholic Church alone possesses, so the Catholic believes, all the "notes" which enable us to distinguish between the Church which Christ founded and its heretical rivals.

The Catholic claims to have proved by pure reason that Christ was God, that Christ founded an infallible Church, and that the Roman Catholic Church is the church in question. Having travelled thus far by reason unaided by authority, it is not irrational to trust the authority, whose credentials have been proved by reason, to interpret difficult passages from the Bible. "The approach to the Church is," as Father Hugh Pope remarks, "through faith in the Bible as a purely human narrative," but, once we have proved that the Church is infallible, we may reasonably accept its teachings on the inspiration of Scripture.

Critics have said that this is a circular argument: "You say the Bible shows that Christ established an infallible Church and that his infallible Church declared the Bible to be inerrant, and it is that inerrancy on which we rely to know that he established an infallible Church. That's going in circles!" No, it's not. This is not a circular argument but a spiral argument. First, as Hugh Pope said, we take the Bible as a "purely human narrative," much as we take Julius Caesar's *Gallic Wars* to be a purely human narrative. We then take the claims of the Bible, with respect to Christ and the Church he said he would establish, and add to them what we can learn from extra-biblical narratives from the earliest Christian years. These show, for example, large numbers of people giving their lives for the claim that Christ was God and proved it by rising from the dead. Not a few of these people knew or learned from the apostles, all but one of whom was martyred (the exception being John the Evangelist). The conclusion reached from this collection of evidences is that Christ truly was God. If that was so, then the Church that he established would have certain attributes, one of them being the note of infallibility: it could make decisions that undoubtedly were true.

One of those decisions concerned the status of the Bible: yes, it was a human document, but it was more than a human document; it was a document protected from error by the Holy Spirit. At this point the argument raises the status of the Bible, which was considered at first as though it were only a purely human document. Once the argument "circles" back to the Bible, the Bible has had its status raised, and it is considered at a new level. Thus the argument is not truly circular but spiral.

> The Protestant reserves considerably more right of private judgment in his interpretation of the Bible, but he agrees with the Catholic in asserting that the Resurrection of Christ may be proved by reasoning similar to that which enables us to prove that Julius Caesar landed in Great Britain. Incidentally, I have now answered your question as to the principle which permits Christians to reject the historical accuracy of Genesis and to discriminate between the story of creation in Genesis and the Resurrection. If we accept the creation story in Genesis, we accept it on the authority of the Church, which has decided that Genesis was inspired, and which has also laid down in what sense Genesis is history and in what sense it is to be regarded as allegorical. But we do not accept the Resurrection on the authority of the Church; we accept it on the authority of human evidence at least as impressive as the evidence for many of the beliefs you, for one, never question.

At times, in question-and-answer sessions, I have followed Lunn's mode of reasoning and have asked how we can know that Abraham Lincoln existed. How do we know that historical references to him are, more or less, accurate and that the sixteenth president was who we think he was? Some in the audience will cite a family tradition: grandfather, when young, had met an elderly man who, when young, had met an elderly man who, when young, had shaken Lincoln's hand. But, I ask, was the hand shaken Lincoln's or an impostor's? Others in the audience will mention photographic evidence. They refer to Mathew Brady's daguerreotypes, which show a high-hatted man standing with Union officers. Again, how do we know this was Lincoln—and that there was a Lincoln? There remain the problems of verification and falsification.

For each of these questions we rely on human testimony and human judgment, and we rely on probabilities. It is possible to imagine how, in theory, a grand conspiracy could have been concocted—but to what end? Why would countless people, in the seventh decade of the nineteenth century, foist on the public a non-existent Lincoln, and how did they manage to effect silence by everyone else, somehow hiding the "fact" that Andrew Johnson's presidency directly followed that of James Buchanan?

I am entitled to my views, and you are entitled to yours, but just as I am forbidden by the laws of logic to support my argument for the Resurrection by an appeal to the "inherent probability" of divine miracles, you are forbidden by those same laws to support your objections to the Resurrection by the assertion that miracles are "inherently improbable."

The occurrence and probability of miracles is the question which we are debating, and we must both confine ourselves to arguments based on historical evidence and not introduce our own *a priori* prejudices under the blissful impression that a prejudice is the same thing as a proof.

I wish that final phrase—"the blissful impression that a prejudice is the same thing as a proof"—could be plastered on billboards throughout the country. Most people work on the basis of prejudice because, sadly, most people can't handle proofs. Many would be unable to draw a syllogism's conclusion even if they were provided two premises. I recall a time when elementary logic courses at least were offered in public high schools, even if not required. Are there any schools that still offer them? Certainly there can't be many, given the widespread inability to parse even the simplest piece of logic.

This sad fact actually offers an apologist an opportunity. His listeners' deficiencies in handling syllogisms will put a crimp on his argumentation. That is unavoidable. He cannot assume in them what might have been assumed in listeners a century ago. But their innocence of formal training in logic makes logical demonstration seem remarkable, even fascinating, to many of them. With patience, an apologist can lead an audience through an extended sequence of logical steps, culminating in an "Aha!" moment for many. Delight in seeing how things fit together sometimes results in some people wanting to learn more, and they go on to good things. They come to realize their own lack and desire to overcome it.

One day, taking a lengthy hike in neighboring mountains, I reached a peak and found there a young couple. They were lost, unsure how to get down and how to return to the trailhead. I showed them the way, and as we descended the young man asked what I did. I said I wrote. His countenance lit up, and he asked for advice. He said he realized that he had been poorly educated—he was a product of local public schools—and he desperately wanted to learn more, but he was unsure how to overcome his weaknesses.

He said he had begun reading Hemingway but found it tough going: there were too many words he didn't know. I remarked that Hemingway commonly is considered a simple writer, at least in terms of his diction, but I lauded the young man for trying his hand at a book he found difficult. He said his real goal was to read *The Brothers Karamazov*. I smiled and told him that Dostoyevsky was far more difficult than Hemingway but also far more profitable since he had a deeper sense of the human condition. Hemingway could tell a good story; Dostoyevsky could change a life.

The young man asked if he could keep in touch with me, in case he had questions as he worked on his reading. I didn't hear from him for months, but then he let me know he was part way through *The Brothers Karamazov*. After that I lost contact with him, but I suspect he has gone on to further rich literature. I should have asked him what spark it was that made him aware of his literary weakness. Something had given him an "Aha!" moment.

> Nor can I permit you to assume that any text which you dislike has been "interpolated." You have got to prove interpolation either by showing that the text in question is not found in an earlier document, or that it differs in linguistic style from the rest of the manuscript, or that it implies knowledge of events later in date than the accepted date of authorship. Proof is what I require from you, my dear Joad. You are not lecturing to emotional moderns; you are debating with a hard-baked rationalist who takes nothing on trust.

By nature I'm a skeptic. Not a doubter, a skeptic. Thus Lunn appeals to me: "you are debating with a hard-baked rationalist who takes nothing on trust." I have no skepticism about the claims of the Church, having had those claims proved to my satisfaction, but I harbor considerable skepticism about such things as "the assured results of modern biblical scholarship," much of which we are called upon to accept on trust. Often enough, "assured results" are indistinguishable from scholarly prejudices. If one's prejudice is that miracles can't occur, one conclusion—drawn by many biblical scholars from the nineteenth century onward—is that the books of the New Testament were written not by the men whose names they traditionally have carried but by much later "schools" of followers who had an unfortunate tendency to imagine things that never occurred, such as divine interventions into history.

I am amused by your lordly attempt to dismiss the Resurrection as unimportant compared with "the highly original and immensely significant ethical teaching" of the Gospels. The message which thrilled the first century was not, as Father Knox remarked, "love your enemies," but "he is risen!"

Your tribute to Christ's "highly original and immensely significant ethical teaching" would, as I have already remarked, be more impressive if you had not attacked, with such persistent vehemence, Christ's teaching on the subject of eternal punishment, on sex, on the conscience (which you describe as "a formidable moral apparatus"), on the supreme importance of the next world, on the comparative unimportance of this world, on the divine value of suffering, and on the fatherhood of God, a God not remotely like your deity but actively interested in every human soul. I agree with you that "for want of attention to his message mankind is in a fair way to destroy itself." I only wish that you were equally convinced of the truth of this fact.

I am glad that you do at least recognise that Christ's ethical teaching is unique. One can parallel certain of his sayings with the sayings of other religious teachers. Doctrines, like men, are both called and chosen, but the unique nature of Christ's teaching, taken as a whole, is beyond dispute. And it is not only the teaching that is unique.

Neither Moses nor Mohammed nor Confucius nor Buddha, nor even Mrs. Eddy claimed to be God. With the solitary exception of Jesus Christ, every prophet and religious leader has claimed to speak as the *representative* of God or of divine wisdom. Jesus alone claimed to *be* God.

And yet this tremendous claim more than half convinces those who, like you, formally reject it. Subconsciously, at least, you hear the ring of truth in the words of one who spoke as no man has ever spoken. Christ was either God or a deluded megalomaniac. You content yourself with a mild criticism of his "aristocratic hauteur." A touch of "hauteur" seems unavoidable in one who claims to be infinitely above all created beings. Even a democrat might forgive the aristocracy of one who could say, "Before Abraham I was."

Here is another characteristically British construction. No American writing today would criticize anyone—particularly Christ—for his "aristocratic hauteur," and no one would reply in terms of even a democrat (lowercased) needing to make allowances for an aristocratic attitude. There still was a functioning aristocracy in Britain in the 1930s, and it still occupied a place of political and social utility. A lifetime later, both the aristocracy and its utility have been hollowed out. (The stereotypic case may be Sir Anthony Wedgwood Benn [1925–2014], second Viscount Stansgate, who refashioned himself as Tony Benn, the better to appeal to his middle-class parliamentary constituency.) One of the delights of reading Arnold Lunn is the cheekiness of his style; at least it seems cheeky today, one might even say counter-cultural. A little counter-culturalism can be a good thing for an apologist, since there is so much in today's culture that ought to be countered.

⁂

You have expressed the most unqualified admiration for Christ's ethical teaching and cannot therefore maintain that those who have patterned their lives on Christ have failed to influence the world. Nor can you deny that in every age there have been large numbers of men who have practised what Christ preached. Surely then it is ungenerous to suggest, as you do, that Christianity has been completely ineffective.

The leaven of Christianity works slowly, and genuine Christians have been vastly outnumbered in every age by nominal Christians whose lives have been comparatively unaffected by the creed which they professed. Any country in which it was fashionable to profess Christianity and dangerous to be an unbeliever would provide you with all the rogues you want for your gallery of eminent Christians.

Even many within the Catholic Church squirm at its history. It's not just that a small rogue's gallery of popes can be drawn from the tenth century and the Renaissance or that the Inquisition, in fable if not in fact, netted innocents along with the guilty. The larger problem is that, throughout the centuries, most believers have believed only nominally. With each generation, the slow process of conversion begins anew and often ineffectively. Only the naïve imagine persistent upward progress, but that is what many opponents of the Church demand to have demonstrated before they are willing to concede much to the Church. It is a convenient way never to concede anything, since persistent upward progress is a chimera—often enough for an individual and always, in the long run, for a society. If it is true that "the poor you always will have with you," it is equally true that we always will have with us, and within us, the sinners.

I agree with you that the Church was very influential in the Middle Ages, but I never suggested that the medieval Church was in a position to impose its will where its will was in conflict with deep ingrained social customs. Theologian after theologian denounced dueling. The Church, which you represent as consistently time-serving, never ceased to insist that dueling was a sin, but the duel continued. Against this failure we may set the success of the Church in abolishing trial by ordeal and in gradually suppressing that plague of the Dark Ages, private war between feudal chiefs. Here again we have an admirable example of the methods of the Church in dealing with intractable human nature. It would have been useless to excommunicate the feudal chiefs, so the Church began by coaxing them to accept a weekend truce. This, the Truce of God, was gradually extended to include Thursdays and Fridays, and finally private war disappeared. These half-tamed barbarians often ignored the restrains which the Church attempted to impose, and often succeeded in imposing, but it is scarcely fair to blame the Church for those incidents at the siege of Jerusalem which should help us to understand the intractable pagan nature with which the Church had to deal.

"It would have been useless to excommunicate the feudal chiefs," says Lunn. There is a modern analogue. It would have been useless to excommunicate Hitler, Mussolini, and other dictators who, in their infancy, had been baptized into the Church. Such men discarded Catholicism about the time they discarded the short pants of boyhood. To them an excommunication would have meant nothing, just as a condemnatory incantation by a Mayan priest would mean nothing to a modern American of any or no religion. The Church always has had to deal with men as they are: recalcitrant, ignorant, violent, petulant. The Church seldom has wielded the sword (and then usually incompetently—an indication that the sword should have been left with Caesar). It has had to rely on suasion, a weak weapon that seldom works quickly and then only on those predisposed to letting it work.

Suasion is the coin of the apologist. An apologetical argument will make no impress on someone determined not to think things through, but it can have some influence, however slight, on someone who harbors a desire for truth. C.E.M. Joad was an agnostic when he engaged in his correspondence with Arnold Lunn, but he was an agnostic willing to consider claims other than his own and not so proud as to stick with a conclusion that had been demonstrated to be false. He ended his life as a Christian, though not as a Catholic.

Joad once boasted publicly that he avoided paying railway fares. In 1948 he was caught on a train without a ticket. He was convicted of fare dodging and fined £2, a minuscule penalty that had enormous repercussions. He lost his chance at a peerage, and he lost his job at the BBC. Humiliated, he saw his health decline, but from personal embarrassment came a repudiation of agnosticism and an acceptance of Christianity. He told the story in *The Recovery of Belief,* published in 1952, the year before his death. I suspect the exchange with Lunn, though it had occurred two decades earlier, played no little part in Joad's transformation.

The Third Day

Arnold Lunn

I sometimes have spoken publicly about what I call the Bing Crosby Church, by which I mean an attitude that was common a lifetime ago, when Crosby played the role of a parish priest in such films as *Going My Way* and *The Bells of St. Mary's*. Those were the days in which, if something needed to be done, a common response among the laity was "Let Father do it." Such-and-so was said to be the responsibility exclusively of the clergy, who had been specially trained for certain tasks even beyond the purely sacramental. Clerical and lay duties—and skills—were clearly demarcated, at least in the minds of many laymen. This included apologetics, which was imagined to be a clerical function. After all, in their training priests studied apologetics. Laymen studied astronomy, anthropology, or auto repair.

Arnold Lunn, writing in the years when Crosby appeared as a priest on the big screen, did not think that way. "The defense of Christianity is left to the priests and to a few eccentric laymen, regarded with good-humored amusement by most of their fellow Christians," he wrote. That should not have been the situation. The generality of laymen should have known their faith well enough, and should have been motivated enough, to take up its defense—and its propagation. "As the elections approach thousands of good Christians, who would be horrified at the suggestion that they should canvass for Christ, will canvass with great enthusiasm for the political party of their choice. 'Nobody is converted by argument' is a formula as popular with Christians as it is unknown among politicians and political canvassers."

Whenever I have spoken about the Bing Crosby Church, I also have spoken in favor of arguing. I enjoy arguing, and I think more people should engage in it, so long as they understand what

I mean by the term. By arguing I do not mean raising one's voice, using wild gesticulations, and picking up the other fellow by the lapels and trying to shake sense into him. That is not arguing. It is a misdemeanor. Real arguing is the calm and reasoned discussion of differences, done in the conviction that truth matters and error injures. Arguing, when done well, can have an elegance about it, like a dramatic performance neatly performed.

For his part, Lunn said, "I have always been interested in the aesthetics of controversy, for controversy is one of the minor arts, and a well-built argument, like a well-built cathedral, is characterized by balance and proportion." The problem, for Lunn and for me, is that not everyone appreciates a well-built cathedral. For everyone who admires Giotto's crucifix in Florence's Santa Maria Novella there is someone who admires Corita Kent's felt banners. It is not enough to say, regarding the fine arts, *De gustibus non est disputandum,* because artistic worth is not a purely arbitrary thing. The brute fact is that Giotto was a great artist and Kent was barely an artist.

Lunn was a great controversialist, but there are people who, if they could be induced to read his books, would find themselves not the least induced to move toward his position. This would be a reflection on them, not on him. He came across such people all the time, particularly those some distance removed from Christianity but not removed from intellection: smart but dumb people who allowed themselves to be ruled by their prejudices. *The Third Day* is a proof of the historicity of the Resurrection, but Lunn had come across many people who refused to approach even the first step, which is to admit that miracles are possible.

> It is this desire to simplify a complex problem, this urge towards a unification which explains the prejudice of the anti-miraculist, for if all phenomena could be explained solely in terms of natural agencies, the task of the scientists would be simplified. The aesthetic criterion invoked in one age to prove that planets must move

in circles is invoked a few centuries later to prove that miracles do not occur, for miracles are untidy and unpredictable intrusions into a neat and orderly universe, ugly discords in the beautiful uniformity of nature.

Historically, this attitude manifested itself in deism, "the belief that God may have created the universe but never interferes in the processes of creation." Consider the English monarchy. "The king of England has a theoretical right to veto laws which have been approved by Parliament. The God of deism has a theoretical right to veto the laws of nature, but neither the king of England nor the King of Kings would be so unconstitutional as to exercise these rights."

The notion that miracles do not happen is more widespread than most people realize. It is a notion held by nearly all Protestants and by many Catholics. They admit the miracles of Scripture but disallow miracles of later times. It is as though they acknowledge that once there was a God who intruded in history and even in mundane events, but that God went quiescent and has become the God of deism in practice if not in theory.

This attitude, which does not differ greatly from that of atheists, makes proving the Resurrection more difficult than one might expect. "It is important to establish the reality of modern miracles," insists Lunn, "before discussing the evidence for the Resurrection, because the principal obstacle to the universal acceptance of the Resurrection is not any defect in the evidence but the unconscious or conscious acceptance of a negative dogma, the dogma that miracles do not happen."

This negative dogma is held tenaciously because those who hold it sense, however inchoately, that they would be inundated if they removed their finger from the dike. "The anti-miraculist," says Lunn, "is more concerned to prove his basic dogma than to discover the truth. He starts from the assumption that as much as possible of the New Testament has to be proved to be spurious and that as little as possible must be conceded to be the work of eyewitnesses. If forced to concede the genuineness or eyewitness authorship of any part of the New Testament he abandons just so much of his theory that he can no longer defend and clings with ever greater tenacity to the rest."

A few pages later Lunn refers to "a learned professor" who "once remarked to me that he found it difficult to believe that a simple and learned Jew [referring here to John the Evangelist] could have written a book which read like the work of an erudite Doctor of Divinity, and yet it is at least arguable that three years in the society of God is almost as good an education as three years at Oxford."

I never came across that learned professor, but I believe I met his children or grandchildren. They are legion, and many of them are practicing Christians. They seem to suffer no particular discomfort in subscribing to a religion the chief claim of which they reject, at least as a historical fact. They seem to think that the Resurrection is all the truer for never having happened. To them, the Resurrection happened in the minds of Christ's followers, not in the annals of history. That is sufficient, and that is as far as they will go.

I often have been frustrated when dealing with Fundamentalists who have inherited misconceptions about Catholicism. Not a few, I suspect, would be willing to give up Christianity before they concede anything to the Church of Rome. There is an analogue among those of no faith and of those of other faiths. Most of these people, wherever they fall on the religious or irreligious spectrum, seem immune to argumentation. They *know* that the other side has no case—and cannot have a case—and that is the end of it. "The real difficulty of the Christian apologist," says Lunn, "is not the inadequacy of the evidence but the invincible prejudice which no evidence can overcome."

Erik von Kuehnelt-Leddihn once commented that of all the forces in the universe, stupidity may be the strongest, but it seems that sometimes prejudice is stronger still. A happy thought is that prejudice has been known to be overcome through patience, kindness, and prayer, which is more, I think, than can be said about stupidity.

Free From All Error

William G. Most

Several years before I entered apologetics work full time I came across books by Fr. William G. Most (1914–1997), one of the most prominent of the (few) conservative biblical scholars in the U.S. This book I found particularly helpful as I was developing my response to Fundamentalists. I made good use of it in the newspaper essays that became the first—and virtually final—drafts of *Catholicism and Fundamentalism*.

Most begins with a story about a Baptist professor, Gerald Birney Smith, who taught at the University of Chicago. Smith gave a lecture to the annual Baptist Congress in 1910. He acknowledged Protestantism's difficulty in determining which books were inspired and belonged in the Bible and which were not and did not. "Luther proposed a practical test," a distinction between books "which have the power to bring men the assurance of forgiveness through Christ and those which have no such power."

As Most explained it,

> Luther thought a book that intensely preaches [justification by faith alone] was inspired, otherwise not. Of course, he never provided proof for such a standard. Nor could it be a standard, for Luther, or any good writer, could compose a book that would preach according to Luther's requirements; yet that book need not on that account be inspired. . . . What Professor Smith demonstrates is that for a Protestant there simply is no way to know which books are inspired. That means, in practice, that a Protestant, if he is logical, should not appeal to Scripture to prove anything; he has no sure means of knowing which books are part of Scripture!

I found myself using a variant of this argument often, particularly in discussions following lectures I gave. I might have been surrounded by "Bible Christians" who insisted that all religious truth could be found in Scripture, if only one were open-minded enough to see it. "But how do you know which books constitute the Bible?" I asked. I never came across anyone so naïve as to say, "Well, just look at the table of contents." Usually the response was that a person not closed to the truth, when reading the Bible, would be "convicted" of its truth and inspiration from the very style and strength of the text.

Echoing Most, I pointed out that many people find certain poetry or modern essays more "inspirational" than they find most of the Bible, yet my interlocutor and I could agree that neither Robert Frost nor Khalil Gibran wrote under a divine impulse. (Gibran was still popular in those days, a holdover from my college years.) On the other hand, some books of the Bible are not at all "inspirational" in the colloquial use of that word. The book of Numbers, for example, reads like dry military statistics—because that is what it mainly is. Unless we were told by some authority that Numbers was an inspired book, none of us would think so, at least if we employed a test anything like Luther's.

Free From All Error is not chiefly concerned with the claims of Fundamentalists but with claims of doubters, Catholic and non-Catholic. Here I mean those who doubt whether Scripture is inerrant. Not a little of this doubt arose in consequence of Fundamentalism. Even today, more than three decades after Most wrote, Christianity, when portrayed in popular media, is portrayed in its Fundamentalist version. Much of that version is refuted easily. When it is, the conclusion is that Christianity has been refuted when in fact it hardly has been addressed. If Fundamentalists seem so evidently wrong on so much, and if they hold to the inerrancy of Scripture, then it is likely that inerrancy either is not plenary or does not exist at all—so the argument is drawn. This is a sufficient argument for the lazy and for those unaware that there is a serious Christianity obscured from view by Fundamentalism.

This book was written for a popular audience, not for scholars. Most could hold his own with liberal exegetes, whether Catholic or Protestant, though he never achieved the visibility that would have allowed him to make notable headway against the novelties in their thinking. At least during the second half of his life he seems to have been relegated to the academic sidelines; probably he would have found it difficult to publish in any of the standard theological journals.

That did not dissuade him from writing for a wider audience, intelligent laymen. For them he laid out the big picture, fairly presented the positions he opposed, and critiqued those positions. I found him persuasive. Later I would go beyond his books, even if I never ventured into the remotest regions of biblical theology.

Much of *Free From All Error* deals with apparent contradictions or apparent impossibilities—Jonah and the whale, as an example of the latter. Most admits that in many such cases we cannot draw a definitive conclusion one way or the other, the evidence being too slight. The book of Jonah has multiple difficult passages, such as the assertion that "Nineveh was an exceedingly great city, three days' journey in breadth." How is this to be understood? On High Sierra trails I have met hikers who covered more than twenty miles each day, carrying weighty backpacks. Are we to think that Nineveh may have been more than sixty miles in diameter? The London of Samuel Johnson's time—certainly more populous than Nineveh ever was—measured only seven miles by two. Manhattan is about the same size.

Most offers several possibilities. He cites a scholar who "suggests that the name Nineveh could have referred to a twenty-six mile string of settlements in the Assyrian triangle." Another possibility was that "Jonah would likely speak at the city gates, where people gathered to converse. As there were many such gates to Nineveh, it would take three days to spend some time talking at each." Perhaps, though when a city is described as "exceedingly great," one generally does not think in terms of the number of gates, since a small city could have many gates, if they were placed in close proximity.

Another issue is addressed. In Jonah 4:11 God says that in the city "there are more than a hundred and twenty thousand people who do not know their right hand from their left." Some claim this refers to babies. That would imply a prodigious population, one that would have exceeded that of any city of antiquity. More likely, the phrase referred to the whole populace, characterizing them as people who could not tell right from wrong.

Most was not a Protestant Fundamentalist; neither was he a Catholic Fundamentalist, in the sense of a Catholic who seems to take his biblical cues more from conservative Protestants than from Catholics. While admitting a certain utility to the historical-critical method of Scripture study, and while seeing sense and nonsense is certain strains of modern scholarship, Most maintained an attractive and orthodox balance. I tried to learn from that as I pursued my own studies, whether of the Bible or of other matters relevant to my work. I regret never having met Most—I have had a disconcerting habit of waiting too long to intrude myself into the lives of writers I have profited from, Frank Sheed being another example—and I regret that a book I found so helpful as this is not widely read today.

Theology for Beginners

Frank Sheed

I made such use of this book and praised it so frequently that I was asked to write the foreword to one publisher's republication of it. In it I quoted from the book's final paragraph, which is worth quoting again: "[W]hat sort of soldier will the uninstructed Catholic make? Stumbling along in the dark not even aware that it *is* dark, half-fed and not even hungry for more, he is in no state to show others the light or the nourishment. Only a laity living wholly in reality is equipped to show it to others and win them to want to live in it too."

That was how Frank Sheed saw things six decades ago. It remains how things are, only more intensely now. In *Theology for Beginners* and *Theology and Sanity* Sheed repeatedly argued that no one can be counted sane who denies the existence of half of reality—and the more important half at that. No materialist is sane, no matter how placid he otherwise might seem, because he thinks there is nothing beyond what the five senses can perceive.

Most Catholics understand this, though most don't think of the question in such terms. They know they have something the materialist doesn't have, an insight that, for whatever reason, was not vouchsafed to him. But how well do they know their own position? How well do they know the basic points of their own faith—enough to explain them winningly to others? Usually not.

I found nothing unexpected in *Theology for Beginners*. Sheed served up no doctrines that I didn't already know, but he served up what I knew in ways I had not seen before and with simple clarity. As I said in that foreword, "Frank Sheed never composed an incoherent sentence." He proved so capable an apologist because he was such a clear expositor. He had read the chief theological works (and not just on the Catholic side of controversies) but made no effort to parade his erudition; looking through twenty of his books, I find only one with more than one or two footnotes.

Theology for Beginners covers the essentials, as one might expect from its title. Sheed first introduces the notion of spirit as distinguished from matter. In successive steps he discusses infinite spirit, the Trinity, the three Persons of the Trinity, and how the human mind can comprehend, admittedly limitedly, what has been revealed to it about the Trinity. Having written about God in himself, Sheed writes about God in his actions: creation, the creation of man in particular, our supernatural life and its undermining through original sin. There follow chapters on the Redeemer, the visible Church, Christ's Mother, grace and sacraments, the Eucharist in particular, and the end of our lives and of the world.

It is what one would expect from an overview of Catholicism: by no means comprehensive, either in its choice of topics or in its discussion of any one topic, but a unity nevertheless. Sheed presents enough for the inquiring non-Catholic and for the Catholic who senses his tenuous grasp of certain elements of the Faith. Sheed "wrote simply, but never simplistically," I said in the foreword.

Each time I read him I am reminded that in this way he was much like Thomas Aquinas. The poundage of that saint's writings scares off many prospective readers: "too heavy—in both senses—for me," they say. But Aquinas makes it clear that his *Summa Theologiae* is for *beginners*. One's first response, on hearing this, is to scoff. The second is to bemoan the decline of education: how much more intelligent the "beginners" of the thirteenth century were compared to those of our own—or even to contemporary readers far beyond the beginner level. These two responses are wrong. The *Summa* truly was intended for beginners and truly is accessible to today's reader, so long as he is willing to enter its reading without fear of immediate discouragement. Similarly, Sheed is accessible to all—and he is blessedly shorter than Aquinas.

I already had the information that was in *Theology for Beginners*. What Sheed helped me see was how to arrange and present that information. He began with asking "Why Study Theology?", the title of his first chapter.

> I cannot say how often I have been told that some old Irishman saying his rosary is holier than I am, with all my study. I daresay he is. For his own sake, I hope he is. But if the only evidence is that he knows less theology than I, then it is evidence that would convince neither him nor me. It would not convince him, because all those rosary-loving, tabernacle-loving Irishmen I have ever known (and my own ancestry is rich with them) were avid for more knowledge of the faith. It does not convince me, because while it is obvious that an ignorant man can be virtuous, it is equally obvious that ignorance is not a virtue; men have been martyred who could not have stated a doctrine of the Church correctly, and martyrdom is the supreme proof of love. Yet with more knowledge of God they would have loved him more still.

This is the sort of paragraph I find attractive in Sheed. He displays modesty but not false modesty. He sees through sentimentalistic attitudes and insists on seeing things as they really are. (As Dr. Johnson said to Boswell, "My dear friend, clear your mind of cant.") Sheed ends up justifying learning more about God, in the process justifying the practice of apologetics. Acknowledging that most men are spiritually starved, he says that if that state is to be relieved, "it must be largely the work of the laity, who are in daily contact with starvation's victims. We must come to an understanding of the great dogmas, so that we know them in themselves and in their power to nourish; we must bend every effort to mastering their utterance. Only thus can we relieve the starvation that now lies all about us."

He continues by saying, "This book will be concerned with theology as meeting the twofold need: the need of our own souls for the food and light and love of God which the great dogmas bring with them; and the need of men all about us, a need which can be met only if we meet it." Thus he gives the apologist marching orders—and not just the apologist but every Catholic. In my early work I took much comfort from such words, especially since, in those years, the 1980s, apologetics existed under a cloud. It was said to be passé, old school, superannuated. It had been dropped from seminary curricula almost universally. Priests even more than laymen seemed to disparage it, but those laymen were hungry "for the food and light and love of God which the great dogmas bring with them."

Catholic Apologetics Today

William G. Most

Fr. William G. Most will not end up numbered among first-rank apologists, but this book came to my attention just when I could profit from it. It appeared as I was putting together the newspaper columns that, when collected and revised, became my first book. It was from Most that I took a formulation that I made use of countless times.

Every Fundamentalist I have dealt with—or so it has seemed—has faulted the Catholic Church for teaching, supposedly, that we are saved through good works. We earn our salvation by what we do. Although I never came across a Fundamentalist who used his name, Catholics supposedly take their salvific cues from Pelagius, Britain's most influential contribution to the roster of heretics. In the late fourth and early fifth centuries Pelagius taught an expansive doctrine of free will: we can lift ourselves by our own bootstraps, all the way to heaven. The good works we perform are done of our own accord and not through the promptings of grace. Credit for them redounds to us alone. His was a heresy that never quite disappeared, and in modern times it has made a resurgence—though not under the name of its founder—because it appeals to those who deny the consequences of the Fall.

In Hilaire Belloc's *The Four Men* (1912), a character called The Sailor sings "The Song of the Pelagian Heresy for the Strengthening of Men's Backs and the Very Robust Out-Thrusting of Doubtful Doctrine and the Uncertain Intellectual." It is a drinking song that begins this way:

Pelagius lived in Kardanoel
And taught a doctrine there

How whether you went to heaven or hell,
It was your own affair.
How, whether you found eternal joy
Or sank forever to burn,
It had nothing to do with the Church, my boy,
But it was your own concern.

The song was not intended to be a just representation of Pelagius, and some of its "facts" were fanciful (there seems to have been no city named Kardanoel, for example), but the song's very existence was a testament to the persistence of a heresy that, without using the term, Fundamentalists accused Catholics of subscribing to.

Although I took the usual route of referring Fundamentalists to James 2:17 ("faith without works is dead"), I learned early on that that scriptural verse failed to make much of an impress on them. A few seemed to be wholly unfamiliar with that book. That might seem unlikely, given that Fundamentalists style themselves "Bible Christians," but many of them read (or study) only those parts of the Bible recommended to them by their preachers. Those who read the whole of the Bible often have little appreciation of the import of some passages, such as John 6, in which the Eucharist is promised and described. James's comment on works is another. "Faith without works is dead" either is passed over or, at most, is interpreted to mean that good works have no significance higher than public affirmation of having "accepted Jesus Christ as Lord and Savior." Doing good works is a good thing—but not a necessary thing.

It was through reading Most that I adopted a formulation that helped clarify the discussion. It came from his making a distinction between the way James wrote about faith and the way Paul wrote about it. They used the same word but in differing senses.

"Is it true that there is salvation in faith alone?" asks Most. "Definitely, yes!" It is "the chief theme of Galatians and Romans." Yet James could write that "a man is justified by works and not by faith alone" (James 2:24)—a seeming contradiction.

Either salvation is by "faith alone," as Luther so imperiously insisted, or it is not; either it comes through faith and nothing else or through faith plus something else. Which is it?

Most made the obvious point that the issue here is with the meaning of the word *faith* as used by the two apostles. The word was not used univocally. James "clearly uses *faith* to mean, narrowly, just intellectual acceptance of a revealed truth." To faith in that restricted sense one needs to add good works. We see this confirmed by Paul himself in Romans 2:6: "He will repay to man according to his works."

Here comes the crucial part. Most says that "Paul does not mean that works can *earn* salvation—but violation of the law can *earn* eternal ruin." Paul does not disagree with James, but he uses a broader sense of faith: "total adherence of a person to God in mind and will. This, in turn, implies certain things." Chief among the implications is that works have a kind of negative role to play in salvation, this being the main takeaway I had from Most. We can affirm that salvation is through faith, but salvation can be forfeited through sin. Salvation is a gift, but any gift can be rejected or returned to the giver. Something taken on by compulsion is not a gift.

Once a Christian is in the state of grace, through baptism or through repentance followed by sacramental confession, he is, at that moment, "saved": were he to die in that state, he would end up in heaven, even if with a sojourn through purgatory. But his state is precarious. There is no adult Christian who has not fallen out of grace through sin. "All have sinned and fallen short of the glory of God" (Rom. 3:23). Someone who has not fallen short of the glory of God, however transiently, is someone who is imbued with God's grace; to fall short is to fall into gracelessness.

The key, then, is not to fall out of grace. This is where works come in, both good works and bad works. Bad works are sins. Through mortal sins we lose sanctifying grace and thus salvation. What about good works? They don't *earn* us salvation but they do something nearly as valuable: they keep us from throwing salvation away. To persist in good works is to avoid evil works, sins. Those who habitually perform good works habitually avoid (but they do not necessarily always avoid) sins that destroy grace.

This was, for me, Most's most valuable point. The Fundamentalist, thinking about Catholicism's insistence that good works are necessary, thinks we believe that we bring salvation to ourselves, and so we are back to Pelagius: "how whether you went to heaven or hell, it was your own affair." The Catholic can answer by saying that good works are shields against bad works. Without good works, there is no prospect that a Christian can maintain grace in his soul, the opportunities to fall from grace being ubiquitous and, often enough, seemingly irresistible. Help is needed if they are to be resisted, and that help comes in the form of habitually performing good works, whether in the form of prayer, almsgiving, or something else.

It wasn't that Most told me something I had not known, but he told it to me in a way that I had not seen before, at a time when I needed a clearer way to convey Catholic teaching to those who were sure the Church was teaching something contrary to Scripture. Already I was coming to appreciate that often apologetics consists of offering spectacles of varying prescriptions to an inquirer. Only one prescription will give him clear sight; all the others will give him at best indistinct sight. What you want him to see—some particular truth of the Faith—will remain fuzzy to him until you come across spectacles that precisely compensate for his particular defect of vision.

Difficulties

Ronald Knox and Arnold Lunn

RECOGNIZE THAT MANKIND IS FALLEN

I never have examined my bookshelves with the intent of setting aside my favorite books. If I were to do so, I suppose I first would place in a pile books that have been important to my intellectual or spiritual development and, with them, books in which I took particular delight. (Sometimes a book would qualify as both.) The result would be a large pile. Then I would discriminate, eliminating books that, however much I profited from or enjoyed them, couldn't make the cut. The remaining books I would cull once or twice more, until only a few lay before me. Those would be my desert-isle books or the ones I might want to be buried with, on the off chance that reports have been wrong and we can take a few things with us.

Undoubtedly, among that handful of books would be *Difficulties*. Of all my Ronald Knox books—I think I have everything he wrote—it is my favorite. (Yes, it is an Arnold Lunn book, too, but the pre-Catholic Lunn.) It likely is my favorite of all the apologetical books I have. It may be my favorite of all my religious books, at least of those not divinely inspired. It is a pity that *Difficulties* has been out of print for nearly my entire life, the second edition having appeared in 1952. If I had plenipotentiary power, I would command multiple Catholic publishing houses (and a few secular publishing houses) to reprint it in suitably handsome formats, and I would command each Catholic household to have a copy, under penalty of interdiction.

Lunn (1888–1974) had broached the idea of an exchange of letters to Knox (1888–1957), saying that in "controversial books on religion there is a strong tendency to deal not with the opponent's best case, but with his second best case." He cited Robert Hugh Benson, "who did produce a book of letters of this description, only unfortunately he wrote both sides himself, with the result that one felt that his doubting catechumen was being rather accommodating in the kind of questions he asked." Lunn would not be so accommodating.

Knox replied in a similar tone. "I think your idea of a series of letters is rather fascinating. I am a little tired of those Catholic propaganda works in which, as you say, one man writes both sides. I have contributed to a kind of symposium—I do not know why it has not appeared yet—in which essays appeared for and against the Church; but as we were not allowed to see each other's essays, I presume we shall all miss one another's onslaughts, like the two armies at Mantinea."

I have to say I like that last allusion. Such things came naturally to Knox and Lunn, their education having been deeper and wider, particularly in the Classics, than was common in any later generation. Well-read readers today are likely to have to look up many offhand references that, for Knox and Lunn and others of their time, were matters of general knowledge. Those same well-read readers might find amusement in something Lunn writes in the preface to *Difficulties*. After making appreciative comments about the civility maintained throughout the exchange, he says, in compliment of Knox, that "[t]hose who agree with me that the Roman Catholic position is untenable have no excuse for believing rather that Roman Catholics are themselves secretly uneasy about their own position." The amusement comes from the knowledge that just two years later Lunn would be received into the Church by Knox and would become one of the twentieth century's top Catholic apologists. So much for the Catholic position being untenable!

Lunn wrote the preface to *Difficulties* and the opening letter, Knox the thirty-second and final letter. The opening paragraph of that letter always has struck me as characteristically Knoxish:

> I traveled in the train the other day with a pertinaciously enquiring infant, the kind that wants to know what everything is "for." At Banbury, seeing the station clock, it [note the older British pronominal usage] asked what the time was; and here at last, it seemed, was a question that could be met with a conclusive answer. But no; on being told that it was ten minutes to two, the little brute said: "What's it ten minutes to two for?" I begin to think that it must have been a relation of yours; whatever answer I try to make, you always start again. However, as this is to be final—definitely Paddington, this time—I will try to make an answer short and clearcut, leaving it to whoever will to judge between us.

At the time of the exchange of letters, Paddington Station was the terminus of the Great Western Railway, which connected London to Wales, Cornwall, and the Midlands.

(When he took the train, Knox commonly worked on the *London Times* crossword puzzle. It is reported that on one occasion, as he held up the newspaper to study the puzzle, a neighboring passenger asked if he could have the paper when Knox was through. Of course, replied Knox, just as soon as he finished the puzzle. In a few minutes he handed the paper to the other man, who turned to the puzzle and found all the squares blank. Knox had solved the whole thing in his head.)

This opening selection is cobbled together from portions of the first and third letters Knox wrote to Lunn.

> I have long thought that the real difference between the Catholic and the Protestant view of Christianity is, or ought to be, this—that whereas we think of the Church as a sort of lucky bag which contains good bargains and bad, people who will be lost as well as people who will

be saved, *real* Protestants ought always to think of the Church as an assembly of the elect. I do not see how a Christian can square this latter view with our Lord's parables, but I see its attractiveness on logical grounds.

Verbosa et grandis epistula venit a Capreis; or, if you prefer it, you said a mouthful. If I may analyse you, I think your letter hangs together in the sense that the whole of it deals with a single subject—i.e. the contrast between the Christianity one finds in the Church, reading through history, and the Christianity one might have expected to find there. But it contains, in reality, three distinct points:

(1) How can Catholics, for so many centuries, have looked on the majority of mankind as lost? (A question not of what Catholics have done but of what they have thought.)

(2) How is the fact of the Inquisition reconcilable with any notion that the Catholic Church was deliberately founded by the Author of the Sermon on the Mount? (A question of what Catholics, as such, have done.)

(3) If the Church is indeed divine, how is it that she has neglected to abolish the enormities of an earlier social system—slavery is the instance you choose, and a good one—leaving it to others, and in fact to unbelievers, to initiate reforms which were centuries overdue? (A question not of what Catholics have done or said but of what they have left undone.)

Let me say one or two things about the general argument before I consider these three points in detail. (I hope you don't mind this pigeon-hole way of approaching questions; it's the only way I can tackle any argument.) I suppose what one expects in such cases depends on the general view one takes of human nature, and perhaps I don't expect enough of human nature. But it is true, isn't it, that if you sit down and think out what you would expect God to have done, you nearly always find it's now what he has done? You may say the Church is not what you would have expected the Church to be; is the world? . . . I only note that it is a fact that on the whole your non-religious man is a more successful reformer, because he can work for the future without worrying over the souls of the people who are on the streets here and now.

The key here, I think, is Knox's focus on human nature: taking man as he is, not as he ought to be ideally (the unrealizable goal of the ideologue) and not even as he ought to be accepting his fallen status and adding to it grace, but man as we actually find him. *That* is the sort of creature the Church has to deal with. Some men, under tutelage of the Church, take the grace that comes to them seriously; most take it nonchalantly and don't do much with it.

The Latin sentence is from Juvenal's tenth satire and translates as "a wordy and great letter came from Capri," referring to an A.D. 31 letter from Emperor Tiberius, who was at his residence on Capri, condemning to death Sejanus, who had become, to Tiberius's thinking, too powerful in Rome. The letter, read to the Senate, rambled for a great while, then suddenly demanded that Sejanus be executed. To understand what something means, it needs to be parsed: that, I think, was Knox's point, as he turned to dividing Lunn's argument into three parts (like Caesar and Gaul, one might note).

⁓ ⁓

With a partial indulgence there is no uncertainty, except for the fact that a humble-minded person may find it difficult to be *absolutely* certain that he is in a state of grace (though of course he makes a prudent judgment to that effect every time he goes to Communion). But to gain a plenary indulgence it is not enough merely to fulfil the external conditions, or to fulfil them while in a state of grace. If you have read your Lépicier more thoroughly you would have found that "affection for a single venial sin prevents the complete gaining of a plenary indulgence." And that is something to chew on. Have you or I ever been in the state named? It is not very easy to be certain about that. The story I have always comforted myself with in this connection is one which I must only use for illustration, because I cannot supply you with chapter and verse for it. It is the story that one of the saints—St. Philip Neri, I think—was preaching the jubilee indulgence once in a crowded church when a revelation was given to him that only two people in the church were actually getting it, one old charwoman and the saint himself. . . .

I should have liked, in some ways, to take up your phrase about indulgences being "deeply imbedded in the structure of Catholicism." That is true in the sense that the doctrine cannot be denied without accusing the Church of error and so making shipwreck of the faith. But the prominence which is given to them in theologies is due almost entirely to the one historical accident that they were the point over which Luther fell foul of orthodox teaching. And the impression which some Protestants have that the idea of indulgences obsesses the Catholic mind and deeply colours Catholic experience seems to me quite false. They are a splendid extra, but still an extra, in the economy of grace.

St. Philip Neri was John Henry Newman's favorite saint. Knox often is considered the Newman of the twentieth century: the pre-eminent English convert and a man of gentle demeanor but sharp analysis. I wonder how often Knox told the story of the jubilee indulgence—and how often Newman told it. The story is a good way to begin a defense of indulgences, which not a few non-Catholics think are licenses to sin or, at best, shortcuts to heaven. As Knox notes, citing Alexis Lépicier (1863–1936)—Lunn had cited the cardinal's book *Indulgences, Their Origin, Nature, and Development* in the previous letter—it is difficult to earn a plenary indulgence, since one has to be without the least affection for even the mildest sin. I suppose many devout Catholics go through life never once achieving even momentary alienation from all sin. This undercuts the notion of an indulgence as a free pass.

> Let me insist from the first that infallibility does not mean what almost all non-Catholics think it does. They seem to think that the pope, like the high priest of the Old Testament, keeps a kind of Urim and Thummin somewhere in the Vatican and that if he wants to know the answer to a vexed question he just applies to this oracle, and the answer is miraculously given him. Every pope, in every decision, makes up his mind as best he can as to the true doctrine of the Church, using every effort to consider the full history of Catholic traditions on the subject. He makes up his mind as anybody else does; the difference is that the pope, in certain circumstances, is providentially directed so that he makes up his mind right. Hence both St. Peter and Pius IX [reigning when Knox wrote] were prepared to "argue the case on its merits."

Even more common than this confusion about the mechanism of papal infallibility is the idea that Catholics hold that the dogma of papal infallibility means a pope can't sin. This mistakes infallibility for impeccability. Impeccability is the inability to sin. Infallibility is the inability to make an erroneous decision, at least in certain highly circumscribed situations. Our Lord was impeccable: by virtue of his divine nature he could not sin. (He also happened to be infallible, of course, for the same reason.) Although the Virgin Mary never sinned and was preserved from every stain of sin, even original sin, she was not impeccable. It was possible for her to sin, had she so chosen. In a loose sense, one could say that she "acted impeccably" even though she was not, technically and properly speaking, impeccable. (Of course, "impeccable," a theological word of art, takes on a quite different sense in everyday conversation. We speak about someone having "impeccable manners" but don't mean by it that he never commits a sin, socially or otherwise.)

What happened, it seems, was that there was much disputing; then St. Peter, exercising his primacy by speaking first, got up, and after his speech all the multitude held their peace. Then St. James, who is generally supposed to have been inclined to the Judaizing party, got up and agreed with St. Peter. Not perhaps in the tone of Bishop [Felix] Dupanloup [1802–1878] submitting to the Vatican decrees, but then (1) St. James was an apostle, and the apostles were jointly witnesses of our Lord's teaching—conflicts about the *tradition* of the Church do not arise while the eye-witnesses are alive; and (2) the whole subject of the decree was rather a matter of discipline than faith or morals.

I think *The Layman's New Testament* is certainly right in saying that the Antioch interview happened before the council. And of course the question at Antioch was simply whether St. Peter should sit at the Jewish table or at the Gentile table; presumably there must have been two because of kosher meat. I have always felt that St. Peter was following the prescriptions laid down by St. Paul in Romans 14:15. But I don't quite agree with you about St. Paul not recognizing the pre-eminent position (at any rate) of St. Peter. The phrase "I withstood him to his face" always reads to me as if there were the assertion of an unwontedly bold action; I mean, it suggests that it wasn't a thing you ordinarily did, talking to the chief of the apostles like that. But it is a thing that can be done in an emergency, when you think the pope is showing weakness; St. Catherine of Siena knew that.

Ronald Knox was famed for his command of Greek and Latin—particularly Greek. He translated the whole of the Bible on his own into what he hoped would be "timeless English." (It turned out not to be.) He wrote mystery novels. They became sufficiently popular that his literary executor, Evelyn Waugh, speculated that Knox's tombstone might be engraved "R.I.P. Ronald A. Knox, Translator of the Holy Bible and Author of *The Viaduct Murder.*"

Perhaps Knox's greatest literary accomplishment was a book almost forgotten now, *Let Dons Delight*, which is set in the fictitious Simon Magus College of Oxford University. On the fanciful date of June 31 the narrator falls asleep in one of the common rooms, dropping off as the dons talk about current events and trends, particularly in religion. The year is 1938. The narrator finds himself waking up in 1588 and every fifty years thereafter. At each half century Knox alters, in strict accordance with contemporary usage, the diction and speaking patterns of the dons whom the narrator overhears. The theme of the book is the gradual dissolution, at the intellectual level, of Christianity in England—the result of separation from Rome—but the marvel of the book is Knox's ability to pull off such subtle and convincing alterations of language. There is no gross jump from the English of Shakespeare to the English of Churchill but a slow ratchet, in fifty-year intervals. (This is another Knox book that is unjustifiably out of print.)

Knox's facility with languages, old and new, made him sensitive to such lines as "I withstood him to his face." Where others would see in those words only a statement of fact—this is what Paul said he did, period—Knox saw a cheekiness, the kind Catherine of Siena is thought to have used in her remonstrations with Gregory XI when trying to induce him to return the papacy to Rome from Avignon. It was this same ability to see in simple things a little more than others saw that led Knox to compose, years later, his only "fantasy," *The Rich Young Man*. Disclaiming anything beyond literary imagination, he worked up a short tale based on the premise that the Rich Young Man was both the Prodigal Son's elder brother and the Good Thief.

By the way, *The Layman's New Testament* (1934) was by the Dominican Hugh Pope. It featured the English of the Douay-Rheims version and cross references on the left pages and a running commentary and notes on the facing pages. Pope earlier had written the five-volume *Catholic Student's Aids to the Bible*. Both works were popular when Knox was corresponding with Lunn.

I think it is a forced argument to imply that because the gospel of the circumcision was committed to St. Peter, and that of the uncircumcision to St. Paul, there were really two popes, one for the Jews and one for the Gentiles. The division is one of missionary spheres (St. Peter up to that time having apparently confined himself to the Dispersion), not of administrative areas. Your phrase "St. Paul never guessed that St. Peter possessed the prerogatives that modern Catholics attributed to him" is one that needs more precision if it is to be answered in detail. Nobody thinks that St. Peter had fans and silver trumpets, and there are obviously a whole lot of ways—not merely confined to externals—in which the pope's position *vis-à-vis* his brother bishops is very different from what St. Peter's was *vis-à-vis* his brother apostles. Especially, as I say, because of the living witness; I expect you know Newman's comments on the point in *The Development of Christian Doctrine*, also because the Church was still too small to need much organization. Yet wherever St. Peter does appear in the Acts, he is always the leading actor in the scene.

This paragraph includes several mini-arguments that I found useful when speaking with non-Catholics, particularly with Fundamentalists who maintained that there could be no historical descent from Peter to today's papacy because modern popes have looked and acted so unlike that "simple fisherman." Knox's response is better than the old chestnut (excuse the mixed botanical metaphor here) of likening the papal office to an acorn (in Peter's time) that develops into a full-grown oak (in our time). I never found the acorn metaphor to convince anyone of anything, perhaps because its use verges on the trite. Even when true, triteness repels. It's much the same with Irish priests' one-time tendency to use the shamrock as a metaphor for the Trinity. If anything, the shamrock—three leaves coming from one stalk—would seem to argue for Modalism rather than the Trinity.

The question whether St. Peter was ever bishop of Rome has always seemed to me an odd equivocation introduced by controversialists. Was St. John ever bishop of Ephesus? I should not have thought that there was any sense in using the word "bishop" as applied to an apostle; surely the episcopate came into being to replace the apostles, and the apostles themselves included the episcopate in their powers as the greater includes the less, as the episcopate includes the priesthood. This, surely, was in Eusebius' mind when he talked about Linus being appointed the first bishop of the Romans. The whole question, I should say, is simply one of names. Wherever an apostle was, in the first age of the Church, he was a bishop and something more than a bishop. Even if Linus was "bishop" of Rome while the two apostles were still alive, you do not surely suppose that he was St. Peter's superior? He may have been thus appointed, though I doubt if Irenaeus implies it; but he would surely be in the position of the cardinal who actually looks after the churches in Rome—I forget his title.

The immediate successors of Peter in Rome were Linus, Cletus, and Clement. Of Linus and Cletus we know little, and we know little more of Clement. We have preserved for us one authentic letter from Clement, written to the Church in Corinth. It is important in the history of the papacy because it shows the Corinthians appealing for judgment to the bishop of Rome rather than to the last surviving apostle, John the Evangelist, who resided in Ephesus. From Corinth to Ephesus it is 350 miles across the Aegean Sea. The distance from Corinth to Rome is far greater, whether one sails around the boot of Italy and up the Tiber or sails to Bari on the eastern coast and then strikes overland. It would have been quicker and easier to contact John, but the Corinthians turned to Peter's successor instead.

If St. Peter was not, at the end of his life, exercising his apostolic functions with Rome as their centre, why did not the bishops of Antioch get hold of this fact and run it for all it was worth? They were constantly jealous for the privileges of their see, and it was common tradition that St. Peter had, at one time, his see at Antioch. No, I think that argument is altogether rather played out. The theory of the early Church, as far as I understand it, is this. A tradition of doctrine has been handed down by the apostles, centred at various geographical points. Each bishop hands on the tradition to his successors (even now, as you know, there is a custom that a bishop should publicly testify his faith on his death-bed), and the traditions of those cities, like Ephesus, where apostles took up their headquarters, are particularly valuable, because there the tradition is likely to have survived in its purest form. But Rome stands altogether by itself, for Rome has the tradition of that apostle who was commanded to "confirm his brethren." Its bishop has a tradition of doctrine which is, by divine guarantee, immune from error as is the general tradition of doctrine collectively given to the Church. Hence when heresies begin to arise, the attitude of the Roman bishop is all-important. I do not mean this is all the early papacy meant, but that, I imagine, must have been its salient aspect.

Peter, whether in Antioch or Rome, never wore a white papal cassock, though he surely wore the tunic that was the historical precursor of the cassock, but then all men of his time wore a tunic. To complain that modern popes have worn cassocks with thirty-three buttons (symbolic of the length of our Lord's life) whereas the first pope never even saw buttons (which, with button-holes, were developed in Germany in the thirteenth century) is to confuse appearance and substance. If Christ gave Simon not just a new name but new duties and authority, those were the essence of what it meant to be the earthly head of the Church. Attire was irrelevant, and attire that alters over the centuries tells us nothing about the existence or powers of the papacy.

A parallel argument, brought up to me more often than the argument from appearances, concerned papal wealth: Peter was a common fisherman, a man of few possessions who lived day by day, yet his purported successors—at least by the time of the

Middle Ages—were men of wealth, political power, and prestige. The discrepancy being so great, these later popes could not have been Peter's successors in any proper ecclesiastical sense. This is an argument that seems to satisfy, so long as it is taken no further. Once one distinguishes between papal authority and papal accoutrements, the argument begins to seem hollow.

> I think I must refer you back to the ordinary books of controversy for Liberius and Honorius. I was always taught (as a Protestant) that Liberius acted under *force majeure*, and that clearly invalidates his expressions of opinion, which he withdrew when at liberty. Nobody claims for the pope a gift of invincible fortitude. And Honorius, so far from pronouncing an infallible opinion in the Monothelite controversy, was "quite extraordinarily not" (as Gore used to say) pronouncing a decision at all. To the best of his human wisdom, he thought that the controversy ought to be left unsettled, for the greater peace of the Church. In fact, he was an inopportunist. We, wise after the event, say that he was wrong. But nobody, I think, has ever claimed that the pope is infallible in *not* defining a doctrine. Your remark, by the way, that it was Athanasius rather than Liberius who saved the Church in the Arian controversy is not in the least offensive to pious ears. It is quite possible for the pope to be remiss about his duty and for God to raise up a saint—witness St. Catherine of Siena again—to hold him to it.

Liberius (reigned 352–366) and Honorius I (reigned 625–638) are the two ancient popes most commonly cited in discussions of the failure of papal teaching, particularly the supposed non-existence of papal infallibility. The one pope signed an ambiguous doctrinal statement, while the other was condemned posthumously for failing to teach clearly and allowing heresy to flourish. It always seemed curious to me that anti-Catholics, particularly Fundamentalists, who showed no particular awareness of Christian history between the close of the first century and the opening of the sixteenth, somehow knew about Liberius and Honorius. Surely it was not from extensive reading of dusty histories. No, they inherited these nuggets of anti-Catholic prejudice from a few nineteenth-century writers whose works still circulated in the late twentieth century.

Lunn, of course, in bringing up Liberius and Honorius, relied on a wider knowledge of early Christian history, though he, too, thought the cases of these popes had probative value. They do, but not in the way Lunn then imagined. As Knox said, Liberius and Honorius (and some popes of later years) could be seen as "inopportunists": they fudged, instead of spelling out Catholic doctrine cleanly. They taught no error, but they erred in not teaching as they should have.

> Now, may I turn your point inside out? Has it ever occurred to you how few are the alleged "failures of infallibility"? I mean, if somebody propounded in your presence the thesis that all the kings of England have been impeccable, you would not find yourself murmuring, "Oh, well, people said rather unpleasant things about Jane Shore, and the best historians seem to think that Charles II spent too much of his time with Nell Gwynn." Here have these popes been, fulminating anathema after anathema for centuries—certain in all human probability to contradict themselves or one another over again. Instead of which you get this measly crop of two or three alleged failures! I don't say that proves infallibility; that would be claiming too much. But surely it suggests there has always been a tradition in the Church—call it an instinct if you like—that what has been laid down by a previous pope is of itself irreformable. And that is the Vatican doctrine against which these criticisms are really directed. One pope who yielded, when he was much in the position of Tikhon with the Bolshevists; one who thought it would be nice if the question of the two wills (much complicated because nobody had yet invented the blessed words "form" and "content") were left an open question—and

then you have to fish around wildly and even dig out
poor old Galileo to make up a party!

This is vintage Knox and another paragraph I often have
quoted. Imagine the popes, "fulminating anathema after anathema for centuries"—usually to little avail, by the way—and all
that pops up, for use by opponents of the papacy, are two curious
historical incidents that prove not much at all. Seen in a certain
light, this comes close to irrefutable proof of the divine institution of the papacy. Any human institution led by "inopportunists" at any stage would have fallen through its own incompetence, but the papacy perdured.

In 1840 Thomas Babington Macaulay (1800–1859), an Evangelical, wrote a review of Leopold von Ranke's *History of the Popes*
for the *Edinburgh Review*. The review contains a long paragraph
that is one of the most remarkable evocations of the papacy ever
composed. That paragraph I often have used in defense of the
institution, for what better defense is there than a defense written
by an opponent? Let me give Macaulay's paragraph in full:

There is not, and there never was on this earth, a work
of human policy so well deserving of examination as the
Roman Catholic Church. The history of that Church
joins together the two great ages of human civilisation.
No other institution is left standing which carries the
mind back to the times when the smoke of sacrifice rose
from the Pantheon, and when camelopards and tigers
bounded in the Flavian amphitheatre. The proudest
royal houses are but of yesterday, when compared with
the line of the Supreme Pontiffs. That line we trace back
in an unbroken series, from the Pope who crowned
Napoleon in the nineteenth century to the Pope who
crowned Pepin in the eighth; and far beyond the time
of Pepin the august dynasty extends, till it is lost in the
twilight of fable. The republic of Venice came next in
antiquity. But the republic of Venice was modern when
compared with the Papacy; and the republic of Venice
is gone, and the Papacy remains. The Papacy remains,
not in decay, not a mere antique, but full of life and

youthful vigour. The Catholic Church is still sending forth to the farthest ends of the world missionaries as zealous as those who landed in Kent with Augustin, and still confronting hostile kings with the same spirit with which she confronted Attila. The number of her children is greater than in any former age. Her acquisitions in the New World have more than compensated for what she has lost in the Old. Her spiritual ascendency extends over the vast countries which lie between the plains of the Missouri and Cape Horn, countries which a century hence, may not improbably contain a population as large as that which now inhabits Europe. The members of her communion are certainly not fewer than a hundred and fifty millions; and it will be difficult to show that all other Christian sects united amount to a hundred and twenty millions. Nor do we see any sign which indicates that the term of her long dominion is approaching. She saw the commencement of all the governments and of all the ecclesiastical establishments that now exist in the world; and we feel no assurance that she is not destined to see the end of them all. She was great and respected before the Saxon had set foot on Britain, before the Frank had passed the Rhine, when Grecian eloquence still flourished at Antioch, when idols were still worshipped in the temple of Mecca. And she may still exist in undiminished vigour when some traveller from New Zealand shall, in the midst of a vast solitude, take his stand on a broken arch of London Bridge to sketch the ruins of St. Paul's.

This is not just remarkable rhetoric. It is a remarkable acknowledgement from a man who was not sympathetic to the Catholic Church. Now back to Knox.

On the infallibility decree itself, apart from the matter of the "ruling decision," I do not think that your objections are very formidable. You repeat, without much apparent enthusiasm, the logical dilemma, so beloved of controversialists, about the infallible pope needing a second infallible authority to decide when he is and when he is not infallible. I expect you are familiar with the speculation, hardly more impressive, "How are we to be certain that the reigning pope was ever baptized?" (We can only have human certainty of this; and if he was never baptized, then his orders were invalid and consequently he is no pope!) What is asserted in the decree is that *ex cathedra* definitions are infallible, objectively; it does not follow that they always can be detected as such. And I cannot understand why we Catholics should need a second infallible authority to guide us on this point; surely here a certainty which excludes all reasonable doubt is sufficient for our purposes? And such a certainty can be obtained, say, in the matter of the Immaculate Conception decree, either by one's own common sense or by the "common sense" of the theologians. I will not labour this point until I know how it strikes you. But if you read any formal manual of theology you will come across heaps of points which, without being *de fide*, are labelled "certain" because the whole tradition of Catholic theology is agreed on them, and no preacher (for example) would dream of teaching the contrary. It is this kind of certainty we should have to fall back on, if we could not decide for ourselves, from the very terms of a definition, whether it was meant to be infallible or not.

But a more serious point arises—the fact that only three or four decisions are recognized as infallible on this reckoning. Your comment is "Infallible decisions are so rare that they have had virtually no effect on the Church's teaching on faith or morals." I agree. After all, there are several organs of infallibility—the recognized general councils, the unanimous consent of the Fathers, the ordinary magisterium (as it is called) of the Church. Thus there are very few subjects on which it would be possible for the pope to make an infallible decision without covering ground which has already been covered by infallible pronouncements from other quarters. The Vatican decree was meant to decide a point of principle rather than to institute a practice. Otherwise, you would expect all the popes since 1870 to have been making pronouncements with violent anathemas attached; we find the exact contrary. The main point is to assert the principle that the inerrancy which belongs to the Roman Church is independent, in theory, of the inerrancy which belongs to the Universal Church; that the truths which have been defined by general councils would have been *de fide* none the less if in each case a pope and not a council had defined them.

Even most Catholics misconstrue infallibility—not just what the word means but how infallibility operates. They have heard of papal infallibility but can't explain, even to their own satisfaction, when and how it might be employed. Many of them are aware that ecumenical councils also teach infallibly (and far more often than do popes teaching on their own), but many are quite unaware of this. And few seem to know the third mode of infallible teaching, the ordinary magisterium of the Church: those teachings that have been taught persistently from the first, even if they never have been reduced to formulas by popes or councils. Non-Catholics tend to muddle papal infallibility and papal impeccability. Few Catholics do that, knowing at least something of papal peccability. For Catholics the confusion lies not so much with the existence of infallibility but with its extent and operation.

If you are content to compare saintly persons who have been Protestants with saintly persons who have been Catholics, like Newman, say, or Pasteur, or Cardinal Mercier, I should fully agree with the comparison and not be scandalized by it. I would be compelled to recognize "religious genius," if that phrase has any meaning, among Protestants as among Catholics. But then, surely, when we have admitted that a Protestant who is in good faith can go to heaven, we have *ipso facto* admitted that he can become a very good man; good, too, with an attractive, dynamic, and infectious kind of goodness. Such a man is, from our point of view, a

Catholic *in petto*, and if he makes a faithful use of such graces and lights as God gives him, I see no reason why he should not attain to greater spiritual eminence. Nay, I can easily imagine that some Protestants I have known, men like King of Lincoln, for example, never had any purgatory. And in common, loose language we talk about such people as "saints," just as in common language we say that somebody's singing is "divine." But Catholic saints, technically so defined, come altogether under a different heading.

"King of Lincoln" refers to Edward King (1829–1910), the Anglican bishop of Lincoln, which once had been John Wesley's diocese. Unlike Wesley, King was High Church. He generated no little opposition for his institution of "ritualistic practices," and he was noted for his mild manner and kindliness. In Knox's view he was a representative *in petto* Catholic, that is, a non-Catholic who was so close to the Church in thinking and practice that he might have appeared to others as secretly a Catholic—precisely the charge that Low Church Anglicans levied against King.

You see, a saint is adorned by God with graces out of the common, for this purpose, among others, that he may demonstrate the divine origins of the Catholic Church. Demonstrate it, not so much to the world at large—many of the moderns would think St. Philip Neri a madman and St. Therese of Lisieux a sentimentalist—but to Catholics themselves. To those outside, uncanonized Catholics, like Thomas á Kempis and Father Damian, can easily be a better advertisement for the Church than some of the saints. But we Catholics expect to find in the careers and in the atmosphere of certain holy people a quality not found elsewhere, which we call by the technical name of "sanctity." And if that quality were to be found among non-Catholics, we should be puzzled, for then it indeed would look as if God meant us to understand that differences of denomination were wholly unimportant. But is it?

I found this an interesting approach by Knox. He seemed to be saying that true sanctity—holiness at the level of the saints—is found exclusively within the Catholic Church, even though we can find quite holy people outside the Church. The difference is not just quantitative but qualitative, and it is a difference that helps us distinguish the true Church from its offshoots.

> I wonder if you agree with me that Tennyson, if he had taken opium for six months on end, could never possibly have written *Kubla Khan*? And yet he was a perfectly workmanlike poet. The quality which Coleridge has and he has not is something which you cannot define or analyse; you cannot even prove its existence to a person who does not *feel* it. So I would say that among the non-martyr saints who have been canonized within the last few centuries—the martyrs are a different category, and we have little material for knowing the inside of the older saints—there is a quality, a touch, which you do not find among the holy men of the other Christianities. Of course, it is possible and quite legitimate to do what I gather your father has done: to isolate those characteristics of the saints which a Protestant public is likely to appreciate in them, to dwell on what is common to St. Francis and Father Damian, to St. Vincent de Paul and Cardinal Manning, to St. John of the Cross and Father Augustine Baker. (You will see that I am only mentioning Catholics; my point is that canonized and uncanonized holiness must have their resemblances, must deal in the main with the same subject matter.) But that, I think, is to miss the most characteristic, though many people would not think it the most important, quality in the saints' lives: the supernatural touch which distinguishes them from other good people, as a piece of music played by a real genius is different from the same piece of music played by an absolutely faultless performer.
>
> It is easy to pick out points here and there which I should call characteristic of sanctity. As, for instance, the desire of suffering. St. Therese's *aut pati aut mori*;

the notion of vicarious suffering for others, as when St. Ignatius stood in the frozen river to save the libertine; a great simplicity, almost childish, as when St. John Cantius ran after the highwaymen to tell them that he had some money after all; a deliberate foolishness, like that of St. Philip Neri changing hats with other people to make passers-by laugh at him; a fantastic reliance on Providence, like Don Bosco's; a desire to run away, even from a vocation which meant untold good to others, such as that evinced by the Curé d'Ars, and so on. It is quite certain that the ordinary Protestant reader would not be edified by such traits, and indeed some of them are traits which nobody would admire in a man who was not a saint. But, for the sympathetic reader, they show up the medium used for the drawing, which is, I suppose, a completely supernaturalized and, if you will, other-worldly atmosphere. And it is not so much the miracles of the saints which impress me as the fact that, when you read the lives of such people, the miracles seem quite in keeping, quite in the picture, whereas in the biography of any ordinary religious leader—say Bossuet—they would somehow be out of the picture. Well, I despair of every making you see what I mean; I am only assuring you that, even to a very unspiritual person like myself, there is an appreciable difference of quality between a saint and a very good person, whether Protestant or Catholic.

What makes the difference between "a saint and a very good person" comes chiefly from the Church being the repository of the ordinary sources of grace, the sacraments, and the guarantor of the whole teaching of Christ. No Protestant church has all seven sacraments (few of them acknowledge that they have any sacraments at all), and Protestantism by its nature is defective Catholicism, with some truths dropped out and other, untrue teachings brought in to fill the gaps. Protestantism can produce the "very good person" but not the true saint. It is as though it can produce a piece of music played by "an absolutely faultless performer" but not the same piece played by "a real genius." The weak of hearing would not notice a difference between the two performances, but those with spiritually sensitive ears would.

Survivals and New Arrivals

Hilaire Belloc

> The curious have remarked that one institution alone for
> now nineteen hundred years has been attacked not by
> one opposing principle but from every conceivable point.
> It has been denounced upon all sides and for reasons
> successively incompatible: it has suffered the contempt,
> the hatred, and the ephemeral triumph of enemies as
> diverse as the diversity of things could produce. This
> institution is the Catholic Church.

With these words Hilaire Belloc (1870–1953) opens perhaps the
most apologetical of his many books. His argument is that "the
situation of the Church at any moment (and therefore in our
own time) is best appreciated by judging the rise and decline of
the forces opposing her at that moment." He divides these forces
into three broad movements.

First there is what he terms the Main Opposition, whatever
is most prominent at the time. Arianism held this role in the
fourth and fifth centuries. Two centuries later it was Islam.
(Belloc did not live long enough to see each of these revive, if
in somewhat different dress.) The Main Opposition will vary
from century to century, and it may have several, seemingly
conflicting parts.

The second group consists of the Survivals. These are "old
forms of attack which are gradually leaving the field." They are
paralleled by the third group, the New Arrivals, "new forms
of attack barely entering the field." The Survivals are losing
influence, but they have some still; their decline lets us see the
weaknesses within them, and those weaknesses may be mirrored
in the Main Opposition, giving us a chance to see how to
oppose it. As for the New Arrivals, they "exemplify the truth

that the Church will never be at peace," and they remind us that every tomorrow will have its difficulties. By understanding the Survivals and New Arrivals, "we can more fully gauge the character of the [Main Opposition], and only in a survey of all three can we see how the whole situation lies."

Belloc finds a poignancy within the Survivals. Just as Ronald Knox, as he wrote his magnum opus, *Enthusiasm*, developed an appreciation and almost a fondness for those he was writing about, wrong as they were theologically, so Belloc has a certain affection for those opponents of the Church who, in his opinion, are fading from the scene. "The old Bible Christian offensive is a Survival pretty well done for. No one will deny the comic side of its exhaustion. The recognition of that comedy is no bar to sympathy with its pathetic side."

Belloc wrote this almost exactly half a century before I first got involved in apologetics. He could not have foreseen the rise of "Bible Christianity," which, by the 1980s, was taking 100,000 Americans out of the Catholic Church each year. Nothing like that was happening in 1930, either in America or in Britain. Fundamentalism persisted then, but it seemed stalled; it made no apparent advance, no inroads. It seemed that the actuarial tables would take care of it, but fifty years later it was thriving, at least in the U.S.

Belloc's next words are ones I quoted in *Catholicism and Fundamentalism*: "There is something very gallant about these literalists. They never retreated, they never surrendered, they were incapable of maneuver, and the few that remain will die where they stand rather than give way a foot. Their simplicity sometimes has a holy quality about it."

While I found the whole of Belloc's book intriguing and even prescient, it was the section on the Survivals that most interested me, because it was such people—not just Fundamentalists but old-line materialists—I had been engaging for a few years. Belloc thought that, of all the Survivals (he identifies five quite disparate movements or tendencies), the Fundamentalist was the weakest, "and its rapid disappearance [is] due to the advancement of learning."

The literalist believed that Jonah was swallowed by a right Greenland whale, and that our first parents lived a precisely calculable number of years ago, and in Mesopotamia. He believed that Noah collected in the ark all the very numerous divisions of the beetle tribe. He believed, because the Hebrew word *jom* was printed in his Koran, "day," that therefore the phases of creation were exactly six in number and each of exactly twenty-four hours. He believed that man began as a bit of mud, handled, fashioned with fingers and then blown upon. These beliefs were not adventitious to his religion; they *were* his religion; and when they became untenable (principally through the advance of geology) his religion disappeared.

A few pages later Belloc concludes his section on Fundamentalism by saying, "The biblical attack on the Church has failed because bibliolatry has been destroyed by extended geological and historical knowledge. It is dying and will soon be dead. But will it 'stay dead'?"

Perhaps not. "The good fortunes of stupidity are incalculable. One can never tell what sudden resurrections ignorance and fatuity may not have. Most of us, if asked to make a guess, would say that in fifty years no odd literalist could still be found crawling upon the Earth. Do not be too sure. Our children may live to see a revival of the type in some strange land."

Fundamentalism did not disappear, and indeed there was a revival in a "strange land"—the land that Belloc's late wife, Elodie, was from: America.

In a later chapter Belloc considers the Main Opposition, which he sees as having three components: nationalism, anti-clericalism, and what he terms "the modern mind," the three "main ingredients" of which are "pride, ignorance, and intellectual sloth; their unifying principle is a blind acceptance of authority not based on reason." This is a telling observation, coming less than a decade before the resumption of the War to End All Wars. "[W]hatever denies or avoids reason imperils

Catholicism. There is nothing more inimical to the Faith than this abandonment of thought, this dependence upon a great number of fixed postulates which men have not examined but have accepted upon mere printed affirmation and by the brute effect of repetition."

Belloc had in mind the *isms* that already were plaguing Europe, even though one of the most virulent of them had not yet (in 1930) achieved political power, but he likely also had in mind the abandonment of reason that had made the Survivals as effective as they had been. Even Fundamentalism had (and still has) a logic of its own, and the overt materialism that still was popular as Belloc wrote, the materialism descended from the Fabians but not only from them, prided itself on its supposed rationalism. Both Fundamentalism and materialism were dependent "upon a great number of fixed postulates," axioms to which no attempt was made to reason. Fundamentalists took *sola scriptura* as a given, something so obvious that argument was superfluous. For their part, materialists began with the proposition that nothing exists beyond the material; with this attitude they saw no reason to deal with the arguments of Christian philosophers.

What Belloc saw in 1930 I saw fifty years later. On occasion I visited the Philosophers Club, the pretentious title of a ragtag group that met monthly in a home in an older part of San Diego. The young host later would become head of a nationally-prominent secular humanist organization, but when I knew him he happily gathered in people who prided themselves on their syllogistic skills even though they never seemed able to draw a conclusion. One fellow spoke darkly about priesthood with all the subtlety of nineteenth-century anti-clericalists. Others, who figured they were smart because they belonged to Mensa, were adept at asserting propositions but regularly were flummoxed when asked to explain their reasoning. I enjoyed the gatherings but learned that people who boast of their ability to reason usually can't.

Belloc was no professional historian, but he was a historian—and a good one. He sometimes got facts wrong. He did not employ footnotes or bibliographies. He did employ his own feet:

before writing about a great battle, he walked the battlefield. He was no armchair historian. His great virtue was the ability to see historical forces from above—no forest-and-trees problems for him—and he understood human nature well, which let him produce fine biographical sketches of key figures, as in *Characters of the Reformation*.

It was partly from Belloc that I came to appreciate the interplay of theology and history, how belief manifested itself in quotidian struggles of individuals and nations, and how religious positions could become fixed as much from historical accidents as from theological ratiocination (Fundamentalists being a good example of this). His writings are no small reason why I have tried to emphasize the historical when making apologetical arguments.

The Church and Infallibility

B.C. Butler

My copy of *The Church and Infallibility* has foxed pages, an inscription from its first (Jesuit) owner, and lots of marginal notations by me. Some books I forswear making any marks in. There have been times when I will purchase a second copy for that, keeping the original copy pristine. But most of my books have succumbed to my pencils.

A single vertical line in the margin indicates something worth reviewing. A double line indicates something of importance. A triple line indicates something I wish I had written myself. A question mark means I wonder whether the writer really meant to say what he seems to have said, and an exclamation point means, usually, that I have stumbled upon a good bad example. All such marks are in pencil, of course. (No one who marks up books in ink should be allowed to have books.) Sometimes, after coming back to a book after a few years, I decide that what I thought was pertinent was not, and the vertical line is erased, or a question mark is replaced with an exclamation point when I realize that, yes, the writer really was that obtuse.

There is no obtuseness in B.C. Butler's book, nor was there any in him. The seventh abbot of Downside, Butler (1902–1986) was a convert from Anglicanism, a Scripture scholar noted particularly for his defense of Matthean priority, and perhaps the chief English-speaking father at Vatican II. He ended his ecclesial career as an auxiliary bishop in the Diocese of Westminster.

I gravitated to Butler's book (he wrote fourteen others plus more than 300 articles and book reviews) because I early on recognized that most arguments against the Catholic faith had to do with the question of authority. On the first page of his introduction, Butler says that *The Church and Infallibility* was written as a response to a recently published abridgement of George Salmon's *The Infallibility of the Church*, which first appeared in 1889. Salmon, an Anglican scholar, was provost of Trinity College in Dublin. (In his early life he worked as a mathematician.) Butler notes that Salmon held that there is "no trustworthy source of obligatory belief except the Bible, and there is no contemporary religious authority that has the right to demand unquestioning assent to its own doctrinal decisions as such."

To me, this always has been the root question, the answer to which answers most other questions in religion. Who—or what—is the authority? Is it a living Church, endowed with a magisterium guaranteed, in some way, to hand on faithfully the deposit of faith and capable of deciding fresh questions in a definitive way, or is it the individual Christian, relying on what appears to him to be the perspicuity of Scripture?

The claim that the Bible is the final authority reduces to the claim that its reader is the final authority. This perhaps can be appreciated best when discussing infallibility. The Catholic position is that the Church itself is infallible and that its infallibility may be manifested in one of three ways: by formal decrees of ecumenical councils, by highly-circumscribed decisions of popes making definitions on their own, and by the centuries-long, consistent teaching of the Church. Protestant churches have no equivalent of the magisterium, even those that have structures that formalistically mirror those of the Catholic Church, such as an episcopacy and councils. If these churches admit infallibility, that charism, by the end of the discussion, is found always and only in Scripture itself. Proponents says that it is the Bible that is infallible.

That is a misuse of the word. The Bible is inerrant—that is, its teaching, when properly understood, contains no error. This is a necessary consequence of the inspiration of Scripture: God could not inspire a sacred writer to propose as true what in fact is false. But inerrancy is not infallibility. Inerrancy is a static thing. It is a testament that both testaments are accurate in conveying the truths they attempt to convey. (An analogy: James and James, the mathematical dictionary, is inerrant in conveying the meaning of the formulas it presents to the readers, at least to the extent typographical errors have been avoided.) Inerrancy is a good and, for the economy of salvation, a necessary thing—the Bible would not be of much utility if it were awash in errors—but inerrancy is not infallibility.

Infallibility is the inability, under certain circumstances, of deciding or defining in error. Infallibility means not being able to make a mistake. Its existence suggests the possibility, under other circumstances, of a wrong decision being made. It is this second status that all of us are familiar with, since we make wrong decisions regularly. It is the very making of wrong decisions that lets us imagine that it might be possible to have a situation in which making wrong decisions is not possible.

Only an active agent can make a decision, right or wrong. To make a decision, a decider is required. No book, not even the Bible, can decide anything. Even an inspired book is a static thing. It is purely passive. It does not have within itself the power of judgment, of discrimination, of reasoning. It may be inerrant, as the Bible is inerrant, but, on its own, it is incapable of drawing inferences from its own text. Something or someone outside the text is required for that. This means that a person may be infallible, or an institution (such as the Church) manifesting itself through one or more persons may be infallible, but no book is infallible.

All this I understood before coming across *The Church and Infallibility*. Butler not only confirmed what I already knew, however inchoately, but he gave me means through which to convey that knowledge to others. In framing his work around that of Salmon, Butler notes that the latter "attacks the Church's infallibility in general and the infallibility of the pope in particular. Broadly speaking, his attack on the former proceeds *a priori*: there can be, he would have his readers believe, no such thing as an infallible authority in matters of belief. His attack on papal infallibility is on the whole *a posteriori*: this dogma can be shown not to have been an original constituent of the Christian revelation, and it is disproved by the fact that popes have contradicted one another. (On this last point, Butler later says that "the cardinal error of Protestantism was to identify development with corruption.")

I mentioned that Protestants, or most of them at any rate, claim to derive their religion from the Bible. Their claim, says Butler, does not match their actuality. "Like Catholics, they in fact accept their beliefs from the tradition and environment in which they have grown up, and they read the Bible in the light of that tradition. What simple, unscholarly Christian in fact derives his belief in the Trinitarian doctrine of the Athanasian Creed from his personal reading of the Bible text?" We all have our popes, and many of them are in our local pulpits.

Butler says that "the *onus probandi* is not on those who appeal to Tradition [here he is writing about the magisterium in general], but on those who affirm that every item of necessary Christian belief is contained as such in the Bible." Just look at the hodge-podge of books that make up the New Testament: "four fragmentary records of Christ's life and teaching," "an inadequate sketch of the early years of the apostolic age," "some letters," and "a prophecy."

> Nothing suggests that this collection of documents, none of which purports to be a compendium of doctrine, contains everything that the Apostles learnt from Christ or that they considered important. . . . [T]he doctrine of the inspiration of Scripture does not involve a belief that Scripture is our sole available source of Christian truth. And, hackneyed though the argument is, it must be pointed out that it is by Tradition and the authority of the teaching Church that we know both the number of the inspired books and the fact of their inspiration.

Scripture, inerrant though it is, is incapable of determining what constitutes Scripture precisely because Scripture, being a book (or collection of books) is incapable of making decisions. Someone or something else has to decide. Only at that point does it make sense even to bring up the concept of infallibility.

In *The Church and Infallibility* Butler talks about much more than this. He considers "the alleged argument in a circle" (that we know the Church is infallible, supposedly, because the Church claims to be infallible), the primacy of Peter, the definition of papal infallibility at Vatican I, and the status of the papacy and the magisterium in general in the early centuries. He keeps returning to the root issue: authority. "How had the Father sent Christ? He had sent him, as Christ's words prove, with transmissible authority. If, then, Christ 'sent' his apostles as his Father had sent him, he sent them with an authority similarly transmissible." The book as a whole is a neat argument, neatly done.

A Handbook of Heresies

Luisa Cozens

This thin book probably did more than any other to generate within me a fascination with heresies—not in the sense of adopting any of them but in the sense of marveling at how many ways there have been to misconstrue the Faith and how those misconstruals have determined the course of Christian history.

In his autobiography, *The Church and I*, Frank Sheed wrote at length about his early days with the Catholic Evidence Guild. Members immersed themselves in Catholic history and theology, and they came from all walks of life. Some were well educated, others hardly educated, at least formally. Some were upper middle class, others were lower lower class. It made no difference. All were attracted to a life of the mind, and nothing was more mindful than the Faith. "We talked theology with one another all the time—at the meal we ate together before the class, on our way to and from the outdoor meetings (some of us spoke at four or five meetings a week)." Most of these public lectures took place at Speakers' Corner in Hyde Park, where a speaker's educational or social background was not determinative of success.

"A powerful theological influence," said Sheed, "was one of the speakers who earned her daily bread scrubbing floors. Louisa Cozens had as gifted a theological mind as I have met. She had only a primary school education but had read and thought and lived theology. From her I first heard Boethius's definition of 'person'—'a complete individual substance of a rational nature.' In a Cockney accent but with an utterly lucid choice of words she told me what it meant." (That is a discussion I wish I had been privy to.)

"In 1928," continued Sheed, "after Maisie Ward and I were married, she came to our apartment after her day's scrubbing (having no quiet place of her own) and without reference books wrote *A Handbook of Heresies*, which is still in print. More than anyone else she helped me to see the value of precision. The last conversation I had with her was on the problem of how the infinite simplicity of the divine mind could know individuals."

That is the extent of Sheed's comments on Cozens. I have been able to learn nothing more about her: what her earlier life was like, whether she ever married, how long she lived, whether she wrote other books. To that last question I suppose the answer is no. If she had produced another manuscript, Sheed and Ward certainly would have published it. From Sheed's phrasing I take it that Cozens did not live past the 1930s; at least he makes no further reference to her, which suggests that those lucid conversations ended far too early. Cozens seems to have been one of those rare autodidacts with whom it is delightful to talk into the wee hours. (Most autodidacts are self-taught so narrowly that their conversation quickly cloys.)

"More than anyone else she helped me to see the value of precision," said Sheed. Perhaps it was because of my own delight in precision that I found delight in her *Handbook*. Throughout my career as an apologist I found precision to be lacking in critiques of Catholicism but also in defenses of it. I once knew an apologist who, despite having studied some philosophy in school, referred to the "three people in the Trinity." I explained to him that "people" is not synonymous with "persons" and that this lack of precision would result in confusion, not clarity, about the sublimest of Christian mysteries. I came across similar inexactitudes by other defenders of the Faith. Perhaps their terminological looseness had no measurable ill effects, but one never knew. As Mark Twain noted, "The difference between the almost right word and the right word is really a large matter—'tis the difference between the lightning bug and the lightning."

A Handbook of Heresies consists of sixteen short chapters, averaging five pages apiece, each giving an overview of a heresy: beginning with the Judaic heresy, which held that, to become a Christian, one had to become Jew first, and ending with Modernism, which, unlike other heresies, did not attack a particular dogma but attacked the very idea that dogmas are possible. The intervening chapters look at Gnosticism, Arianism, Nestorianism, Pelagianism, Protestantism, and other departures from orthodoxy. An appendix of nine pages outlines nine "lesser heresies."

In her introduction Cozens says that the "little band which Christ had formed and trained" went forth, after the descent of the Holy Spirit at Pentecost, "to bring all minds into captivity to the truth." The minds they met "were not minds empty, waiting passively for the truth, but minds already active, with ideas, theories, and habits of thought of their own." The truth entered minds receptive to it but already influenced by other ideas, some of which were inimical to the truth and others of which were not easily made to co-exist with it. So it would be throughout Christian history.

Heresies come and go in their outer manifestations, but their principles seem to undergo constant resurrection. In her chapter on Gnosticism, Cozens says this about a later revivification of that heresy, Albigensianism:

> The Albigenses, whom many people imagine as precursors of Evangelical Pietism, taught a peculiarly poisonous, because peculiarly practical, variant of the same heresy. Holding matter, and the life of the senses bound up with matter, to be altogether evil, they considered marriage and procreation essentially wrong and, therefore, abortion and sometimes suicide commendable: nor in extreme cases did they hesitate to allow a certain practical assistance from their initiates to a neophyte who shrank at the last moment from this supremely logical conclusion.

Today we see a successor to this attitude among those for whom marriage is nothing more than a contract (breakable at will), for whom an unborn child is an expendable inconvenience, and for whom there is no higher last goal than leaving this life by means of an injection (sometimes given with "a certain practical assistance"). Those who redefine or ignore marriage and who endorse abortion and euthanasia usually are not thought of as Christian heretics—many of them never have been Christians in any sense—but they nevertheless are heirs to the remnants of Christian civilization, against which they remain in unconscious rebellion. If ancient Gnostics and medieval Albigenses were to materialize on our streets, they not only would recognize one another as ideological kin but would find that the beliefs that made them notorious centuries ago make others honored today.

Sheed mentioned precision. Perhaps there is no better example of precision's importance than the Council of Nicaea, which convened in 325. That council sought to settle the proper way to understand the relationship between the Father and the Son. Was the latter of one substance with the former, or was he only of like substance? The Greek term of art for "of one substance" is *homoousion*, the term for "of like substance" *homoiousion*. They differ by a single *iota*, the smallest of the Greek letters.

The Arians, against whom the council was called, did not believe in Christ's divinity but believed him to be the greatest of all creatures. He was not of the *same* substance as the Father but of a *like* substance, they said, not uncreated but created. Their defenders at the council argued for *homoiousion* as a term that would satisfy all parties. Besides, they asked, what difference would a mere iota make? From this we get a saying used to resolve unimportant disputes: "There's not an iota of difference between them."

In fact, that tiny letter made the difference between Christianity and non–Christianity. Christianity holds that Christ is divine. Non-Christianity admires him as a prophet and wonderworker but not as God. To settle on *homoiousion* would have been to settle on a new religion. It would have been a denial of Christ's identity. Cozens mentions "the well-known sneer" that "the whole Christian world convulsed about a diphthong. How little they realized that on that one diphthong depended the whole Christian Faith."

So it is today. We live in an age in which precision not only is not valued but is feared because it delineates. It says, "On this side, truth; on that side, error." A lack of precision, or a disregard of precision, says truth and error are just not that important, so let's get on with life. This is an attitude that I have met innumerable times as an apologist: fear of the consequences of saying yes for yes and no for no.

19

No Popery

Herbert Thurston, S.J.

It hardly was surprising that the Protestant Reformation should spawn anti-Catholic prejudice, but it may seem strange that the most persistent anti-Catholicism has been found not in Luther's Germany or Calvin's Geneva but in Anglican England. The surprise comes from Anglicanism's being less of a split from Catholicism than is either Lutheranism or Calvinism. One might expect that the broader the heresy, the sharper the antagonism, but that was not how things turned out. Nowhere in continental Europe was hostility by Reformers as sharp as it was in Elizabethan and post-Elizabethan England. Catholics were better off in Presbyterian Scotland—which maintained a sufficiently large Catholic population to afford support for the Old and Young Pretenders—than they were south of Hadrian's Wall. Catholic emancipation was not substantially fulfilled until the Relief Act of 1829. Even then many Protestants in Great Britain remained deeply prejudiced against "Papistry."

Just over a century after the Relief Act, Herbert Thurston (1856–1939), a Jesuit priest (how appropriate, given centuries-long railing against that order), wrote a book that examined, in minute detail, many of the chief historical arguments against the Catholic Church, as given in the popular press. His preface begins with the droll reminder that, in the original Litany of the Book of Common Prayer, congregants were expected to pray: "From the tyranny of the Bishop of Rome and all his detestable enormities, good Lord deliver us." That line was removed early on, but its spirit remained in such works as *Foxe's Book of Martyrs*, which still was circulated widely in Thurston's day and is on the shelves of not a few American Fundamentalists even today.

Thurston prefaces his book with a quotation from John Galsworthy's novel *The Silver Spoon*:

> "But you don't suppose," said Michael, "that people would believe a thing like that."
>
> "They will believe anything, my dear, that suggests corruption in public life. It's one of the strongest traits in human nature. Anxiety about the integrity of public men would be admirable, if it wasn't so usually felt by those who have so little integrity themselves that they can't give others credit for it."

Thurston says, "I have wished primarily to illustrate the principle [Galsworthy] enunciates that there is nothing which people will not believe about a public man and moreover to show that this is particularly verified when that public man succeeds to a load of inherited obloquy such as is the case with all the popes." He acknowledges that there can be "no question of maintaining that the record of the papacy is unsullied. There have been popes whose private lives and even public conduct have brought disgrace upon the sublime office which they held." But those are exceptional cases. On the whole, the popes have been an impressive lot, fulfilling their duties better than one might expect. About most of the popes of the last four centuries almost nothing derogatory can be said—at least not said factually and legitimately.

That has not stopped anti-Catholics, who have shown as little deference to modern popes as to medieval or ancient popes. In sixteen chapters Thurston looks at many of the charges that formed the prejudice found in so many British minds. He notes that many papal critics, although not bad men themselves, fail to recognize their own bias and think themselves to be moderate when condemning various historical episodes. "The tendency of the biased critic, writing years after the event, even when honest in his intention, is to treat such slanders as exaggerations rather than as inventions and to assume that truth is best attained by steering a middle course between panegyric and denunciation."

I found this often enough in my own experience. In the early years of my work as an apologist, I focused chiefly on the Fundamentalist attack on Catholicism, partly because it was more prominent than it is today and partly because I was fascinated by the mental machinations required to make the anti-Catholic case. Not a few times an opponent of the Church—and particularly of the papacy—acknowledged that people such as Jack Chick (in his grotesque comic books) or Tony Alamo (in his conspiratorial imaginings) admittedly were crude and, mostly, wrong, but their very obtuseness suggested that "mainstream" anti-Catholics such as Bartholomew F. Brewer or Loraine Boettner must have gotten the story more or less right. After all, the Brewers and Boettners disavowed the Chicks and Alamos, which suggested a level of competence and reliability among the former. Catholics may not have slain their tens of thousands, but surely it followed that they had slain their thousands. And yet they didn't, at least not in the cases at hand.

On many topics Thurston provided me with handy formulations of things I knew but could not express as well as he. In his chapter on "The Popes and the Bible," he notes, "Down to the end of the Middle Ages everywhere, and in Southern Europe very much longer, the man who was able to read at all was able to read Latin, and roughly at least to understand it. What is so constantly overlooked is the fact that every child who was taught to read had his first lessons, not in his own vulgar tongue, but in Latin. He began with the *Pater noster*, the *Ave*, the *Credo*, and a few of the psalms. The elementary school-books printed in England at the beginning of the sixteenth century prove this clearly." This sort of historical tidbit I found handy.

Thurston deals not only with anti-Catholics who evince not only little knowledge of history but little education on their own part; he also deals with prominent anti-Catholic scholars such as G.G. Coulton, who lectured at Cambridge and who perhaps became best known, in the 1930s, through his frequent journalistic encounters with Hilaire Belloc. The two men seemed to have approximately equal disdain for one another. In *No Popery*

Thurston takes up a paragraph from Coulton's *Anglican Essays*, in which he claimed:

> In the third Canon of that Council is enacted that bishops should inquire at least once a year in every parish, with power, if need be, to compel the whole community on oath to name any heretics whom they knew. . . . For the heretics themselves, they are to be "exterminated," and any prince neglecting to exterminate them is to be deposed by the pope, who will release his subjects from their allegiance.

This is a charge that I have come across in more recent Fundamentalist literature. Thurston handles it deftly. He notes that in the original Latin text that Coulton refers to (but doesn't quote), the word *exterminari*, when standing alone, does not necessarily mean to kill someone. It often means to send a person away—into the "external." Thurston cites a medieval regulation concerning fasting: If someone breaks a Lenten fast, "let him do penance for a year. But if he frequently does this and it has become habitual with him, let him be put out of every church [*exterminari ab omni ecclesia*]." Thurston says, "Now it is quite impossible to believe than any death penalty was imposed for a breach of the law of fasting, and in fact we frequently find the same canon with a change of wording—*saparetur*, let him be excluded from every church. Here, then, is proof positive that in ecclesiastical legislation *exterminari* does not mean 'killed.'"

To make the point even more obvious, Thurston quotes a letter from Pope Innocent III to the king of Aragon. The pope says that heretics who wish to return to the Faith may be reconciled by their bishops, but those who are contumacious are to be "exterminated" from their cities and they are not to be readmitted unless they can give proof of their adherence to orthodoxy. "It is hard to see," concludes Thurston, "how even Dr. Coulton can suppose that a man who has been exterminated by death should be able afterwards to repent and be allowed to return to his home again."

It is precision such as this—a trait evident throughout Thurston's writing—that I found both attractive and useful, though I rarely found myself in a position to need to go to the sources as did Thurston. If nothing else, his book put me on notice that even well-educated and, apparently, well-disposed people could be convinced of the duplicity or mendacity of the papacy because they somehow got hold of an argument that seems neither benighted nor unfair, however unflattering it may be to the Church or to its temporal leader. If a G.G. Coulton could convince himself of the worth of a particular anti-Catholic claim, would it be a surprise for his readers to follow his lead?

20

An Essay on the Development of Christian Doctrine

John Henry Newman

ONLY CATHOLICISM STANDS UP TO THE TEST OF HISTORY

In 1995 I was in the Twin Cities for the convention of the Fellowship of Catholic Scholars. I found myself with free time and drove to Stillwater, Minnesota, home of Loome Theological Booksellers, hoping to find one or two volumes to take back with me. I found thirty-five: the most handsome set of the works of John Henry Newman (1801–1890) that I'd ever seen. The books were published in the 1870s by four houses: Longmans, Green, Reader, and Dyer; Burns and Oates; Rivingtons; and Basil Montagu Pickering. They published in parallel, in total about four volumes per year. The volumes are uniform: thick boards, ribbed spines with gold leaf, patterned covers matched by the endpapers and by the edges on all three sides of the pages. Some pages are foxed, but most are clean. The typesetting is of the highest quality. The only defect in the set is that it is missing the first volume of the three-volume *Historical Sketches*. Oh, Vol. I is there all right, but only apparently; the text inside is a duplicate of Vol. III. Otherwise, the set is near-perfect. I consider it my pearl of great price, even though I didn't have to sell all I had to acquire it.

I have yet to read the whole of Newman's corpus and hope that my departure may be delayed until I do, so that I may enter the next world not quite as ignorant as I find myself still to be.

I suspect that when my end comes, one of my chief regrets will be not having read more assiduously. Certainly I will regret not having gotten to all the books in my library, not just the Newman titles but many others.

Most Americans would consider me a bookworm. I consider myself more a bookslug. Since 1982 I have kept a log of all the books I have finished reading. The operative word is "finished." No book is entered into the log until I have read it all the way through, excepting perhaps notes and indices. A book that is skimmed is a book that doesn't make the cut. Likewise a book all of which has been read except the last chapter.

When I view my bookshelves, I find many books with bookmarks proclaiming where I failed to finish them off. Some years I have read partially as many books as I have read completely. In my best years I read completely about a hundred books, but my best years are few. In my worst years the number of books read is too low for me to admit in public. The problem is that I am a slow reader—but deliberately slow. I want to savor the words, not rush past them. I want to give them due respect. When young, I took a speed-reading course and marveled at how quickly I could finish a book at 2,000 words per minute, but I soon applied the brakes. A landscape can be appreciated when walked through on a path but not when driven past on a freeway.

Long before I visited Loome's I bought a copy of Newman's *Essay on the Development of Christian Doctrine*, published as a Penguin paperback in 1974. I still have it and enjoy flipping through the pages to see where my younger self made penciled notations in the margins. I don't know whether to be gratified or dismayed at realizing I would make the same marks today as I did more than four decades ago. I like to think this suggests early advance rather than late decline. However that may be, Newman's *Essay* proved pivotal for me in that it cemented in my mind the importance of the historical approach to apologetics. Most Catholic apologists, when dealing with challenges to the Faith from Protestantism, don't venture far from arguments based on Scripture, on the presumption that non-Catholics won't be influenced by any other sort of argument. Newman demonstrated to me that this is a shortsighted approach. The whole argument of the *Essay* is historical. Hardly a sentence depends on construing a biblical passage.

> [S]ome writers have gone on to give reasons from history for their refusal to appeal to it. They say that, when they come to look into the history of Christianity, they find its doctrines so variously represented, and so inconsistently maintained by its professors, that, however natural it be *a priori*, it is useless, in fact, to seek in history the matter of that Revelation which has been vouchsafed to mankind; that they cannot be historical Christians if they would. They say, in the words of [William] Chillingworth [1602–1644], "There are popes against popes, councils against councils, some fathers against others, the same fathers against themselves, a consent of fathers of one age against a consent of fathers of another age, the Church of one age against the Church of another age."
>
> And it must be allowed to such persons that, while reason antecedently suggests an historical inquiry, as the means of arriving at a knowledge of Christianity, it makes no promise that difficulties will not embarrass its course, or even preclude its satisfactory completion. The remoteness or nearness of the times, the scantiness or the abundance of materials, the multitude of details, the depth and intricacy of the system, the subtle intermixture of received teaching and personal opinion, and the disorder which is inevitable in any mass of historical facts—the problem of finding a point of view from which minds born under the gracious shelter of Revelation may approximate to an external and general survey of it—these are considerations which lead to many misgivings, that, even though history be the true mode of determining the character of Christianity, still it cannot be satisfactorily used for the purpose.

Newman's style differs markedly from that of Samuel Johnson, but I can't help but think of the good Doctor when reading "it makes no promise that difficulties will not embarrass its course": "embarrass" is a Johnsonism if there ever was one. Johnson and Newman, the two great literary figures of their times, argued not so much through syllogisms but through spirals: they often approached their target at a distance, circling it ever more closely as they built up the evidences and eliminated alternatives. Rhetoric is the art of persuasion. Sometimes a single syllogism is enough to turn a mind, but more commonly mental conversion requires a skein of evidences, no single one of which is determinative but which, when taken together, point to an inescapable conclusion.

> Now it cannot be denied that this anticipation is in a measure, though only in a measure, fulfilled. It is not fulfilled in such a sense that an inquirer, coming to history, would not obtain a certain definite impression what Christianity was, and certain general views of its doctrines, principles, and characteristics. The nature and temper of the religion, as a matter of fact, no one can mistake, whether he accept it or stumble at it. No one, for instance, will say that Christianity has not always taught benevolence and mercy; that it has sanctioned injustice, or made light of impurity; that its spirit has been sceptical; that it has discountenanced what is called the sacramental principle, or the principle of mystery. Bold outlines, which cannot be disregarded, rise out of the records of the past, when we look to see what it will give up to us: they may be dim, they may be incomplete, but they are definite; there is that which they are not, which they cannot be. Whatever be historical Christianity, it is not Protestantism. If ever there were a safe truth, it is this.

This is one of the most memorable—and most remembered—lines Newman ever wrote: "Whatever be historical Christianity, it is not Protestantism. If ever there were a safe truth, it is this." There is no indirection here, no compromise. Newman, a one-time Protestant, is as blunt as can be, and that makes him refreshing. He completes his thought:

And Protestantism has ever felt it. I do not mean that every Protestant writer has felt it, for it was the fashion at first, at least as a rhetorical argument against Rome, to appeal to past ages, or to some of them, but Protestantism, as a whole, feels it and has felt it. This is shown in the determination already referred to, of dispensing with historical Christianity altogether, and of forming a Christianity from the Bible alone: men never would have put it aside, unless they had despaired of it. It is shown by the long neglect of ecclesiastical history in England, which prevails even in the English Church. Our popular religion scarcely recognizes the fact of the twelve long ages [centuries] which lie between the Councils of Nicaea and Trent, except as affording one or two passages to illustrate its wild interpretations of certain prophecies of St. Paul and St. John. It is melancholy to say it, but the chief, perhaps the only, English writer who has any claim to be considered an ecclesiastical historian is the infidel Gibbon. . . .

And the utter incongruity between Protestantism and historical Christianity is true whether the latter be regarded in its earlier or in its later centuries. Protestants can as little bear its ante-Nicene as its post-Tridentine period.

In earlier times Protestant controversialists appealed to history, says Newman, but that soon proved fruitless: "men never would have put [history] aside, unless they had despaired of it." This is a truth I have seen confirmed repeatedly. Fundamentalist and Evangelical apologists almost never make the slightest referral to history, at least not that history lying between the closing of the first century and the opening of the sixteenth. True, they bring up the Inquisition and the "bad popes" of the tenth century—those are easy targets—but otherwise they have little to say about Christianity as it was believed and lived for a millennium and a half. If the eighteenth century saw in American Protestantism a Great Awakening, for that much longer period there was a Great Forgetting.

That Protestantism, then, is not the Christianity of history, it is easy to determine, but there is a determination which is difficult. It is difficult to complete, to finish from history that picture of the divine religion which, even in its outlines, is sufficient to condemn Protestantism, though not sufficient to imprint upon our minds the living image of Christianity. Confused, inaccurate knowledge is no knowledge. It is the very fault we find with youths under education that they use words without meaning, that they are wanting in precision and distinctness, that they are ignorant what they know and what they do not know. We account this a great defect of mind, which must be overcome. Now our difficulty lies in getting beyond this half knowledge of Christianity, if we make history our teacher; in obtaining from it views serviceable, ready, for belief, and practice, whole views, definite answers to definite questions, critical decisions between truth and error, explanations of its own variations, measures of its meaning. History is not a creed or a catechism; it gives lessons rather than rules; it does not bring out clearly upon the canvass the details which were familiar to the ten thousand minds of whose combined movements and fortunes it treats. Such it is from its very nature; nor can the defect ever fully be remedied. This must be admitted; at the same time, principles may be laid down with considerable success as keys to its various notices, enabling us to arrange and reconcile them.

Newman refers to the students of his time as "wanting in precision and distinctness." The implication is that the problem was not as evident in their elders. What may have been true in 1845, when the *Essay* was published, doesn't seem so true today. Today's apologist needs to work from the supposition that nearly all of his readers or listeners are "wanting in precision and distinctness": the result of six generations of educational decline. In Newman's time most people, and certainly all educated people, could be expected to know at least the outlines of the history of Western civilization. That has ceased to be the cases in our presentist culture.

The following Essay is directed towards a solution of
the difficulty which has been stated—the difficulty
which lies in the way of using the testimony of our
most natural informant concerning the doctrine and
worship of Christianity, viz. the history of eighteen
hundred years. The view on which it is written has at all
times, perhaps, been implicitly adopted by theologians,
and, I believe, has recently been illustrated by several
distinguished writers of the continent, such as [Joseph]
De Maistre [1753–1821] and [Johann Adam] Möhler
[1796–1838]: viz., that the increase and expansion of
the Christian creed and ritual, and the variations which
have attended the process in the case of individual
writers and churches, are the necessary attendants on
any philosophy or polity which takes possession of the
intellect and heart and has had any wide or extended
dominion; that, from the nature of the human mind, time
is necessary for the full comprehension and perfection
of great ideas, and that the highest and most wonderful
truths, though communicated to the world once for all
by inspired teachers, could not be comprehended all at
once by the recipients but, as received and transmitted
by minds not inspired and through media which were
human, have required only the longer time and deeper
thought for their full elucidation. This may be called
the *Theory of Development.*

An error common to conservative Protestants is imagining
that Christian doctrines arrived fully formed. The corresponding (and more dangerous) error on the part of theologically liberal Protestants and their Catholic counterparts is imagining
that doctrines perpetually evolve and so ultimately lack fixity:
what is true today may not be true tomorrow. Newman rejected
both the static and the evolutionary views of doctrines. By *development* he meant the deepening understanding and working out
of beliefs so that they became better understood in themselves
and in their logical implications. (Aquinas was an excellent example of this logical working-out, though Newman hardly ever
mentions him.)

[I]f Protestantism were said to lie in its theory of private judgment, and Lutheranism in its doctrine of justification, this would be an approximation to the truth, but it is plain that to argue or to act as if these were adequate definitions would be a serious mistake. Sometimes an attempt has been made to ascertain the "leading idea," as it has been called, of Christianity; a remarkable essay as directed towards a divine religion, when, even in the existence of the works of man, the task is beyond us. Thus, the one idea of the Gospel has been decided by some to be the restoration of our fallen race, by others philanthropy, by others the spirituality of true religious service, by others the salvation of the elect, by others the union of the soul with God. All these representations are truths, as being aspects of Christianity, but none of them is the whole truth. For Christianity has many aspects: it has its imaginative side, its philosophical, its ethical, its political; it is solemn, and it is cheerful; it is indulgent, and it is strict; it is light, and it is dark; it is love, and it is fear.

The final sentence of this paragraph is another one worth noting. Too often Christians speak of their faith as being all this way or all that way. If Christianity is only love, without fear of damnation or fear of the Lord, the result is a syrupy "Jesus is my friend" religion that withers when faced with adversity. If Christianity is only strict and never indulgent, it smothers nascent conversions and turns in upon itself.

Principle is a better test of heresy than doctrine. Heretics are true to their principles, but change to and fro, backwards and forwards, in opinion; for very opposite doctrines may be exemplifcations of the same principle. Thus the Antiochenes and other heretics sometimes were Arians, sometimes Sabellians, sometimes Nestorians, sometimes Monophysites, as if at random, from fidelity to their common principle, that there is no mystery in theology. Thus Calvinists become Unitarians from the principle of private judgement. The doctrines of heresy are accidents and soon run to an end; its principles are everlasting.

This, too, is often the solution of the paradox "Extremes meet," and of the startling reactions which take place in individuals, viz., the presence of some one principle or condition, which is dominant in their minds from first to last. If one of two contradictory alternatives be necessarily true on a certain hypothesis, then the denial of the one leads, by mere logical consistency and without direct reasons, to a reception of the other. Thus the question between the Church of Rome and Protestantism falls in some minds into the proposition, "Rome is either the pillar and ground of the Truth or she is Antichrist"; in proportion, then, as they revolt from considering her the latter are they compelled to receive her as the former.

The Catholic writer Erik von Kuehnelt–Leddihn (1909–1999) repeatedly argued that extremes never meet: extremely hot and extremely cold, extremely large and extremely small, extremely wise and extremely stupid. Often, he said, what appear to be opposite extremes are not really opposites but are variants of the same underlying principle. It has been a common error to say that Soviet Communism and Nazism were at the extreme ends of the political spectrum from one another. Kuehnelt-Leddihn saw them as rising from the same erroneous view of human nature, which meant they prescribed similar erroneous solutions, with one manifesting itself as international socialism and the other as national socialism—in either case, socialism. So it has been in Church history. Movements that warred against one another ("warred" either figuratively or literally), especially in the early Church, usually were not so much opponents as competitors. They held the same underlying principles and seemed to represent extreme ends of the religious spectrum only because they opposed one another with ferocity.

A true development, then, may be described as one which is conservative of the course of development which went before it, which is that development and something besides; it is an addition which illustrates, not obscures, corroborates, not corrects, the body of thought from which it proceeds; and this is its characteristic as contrasted with a corruption.

For instance, a gradual conversion from a false to a true religion, plainly, has much of the character of a continuous process, or a development, in the mind itself, even when the two religions, which are the limits of its course, are antagonistic. Now let it be observed that such a change consists in addition and increase chiefly, not in destruction. [Next Newman quotes himself, from *Tract 85*, written in 1838 while he was part of the Oxford Movement within the Anglican Church.] "True religion is the summit and perfection of false religions; it combines in one whatever there is of good and true separately remaining in each. And in like manner the Catholic creed is for the most part the combination of separate truths, which heretics have divided among themselves, and err in dividing. So that, in matter of fact, if a religious mind were educated in, and sincerely attached to some form of heathenism or heresy, and then were brought under the light of truth, it would be drawn off from error into truth, not by losing what it had but by gaining what it had not, not by being unclothed but by being 'clothed upon,' 'that mortality may be swallowed up of life.' That same principle of faith which attached it to its original wrong doctrine would attach it to the truth, and that portion of its original doctrine, which was to be cast off as absolutely false, would not be directly rejected but indirectly, *in* the reception of the truth which is its opposite. True conversion is ever of a positive, not a negative, character."

Such too is the theory of the Fathers as regards the doctrines fixed by councils, as is instanced in the language of St. Leo, "To be seeking for what has been disclosed, to reconsider what has been finished, to tear up what has been laid down, what is this but to be unthankful for what is gained?" Vincent of Lerins, in like manner, speaks of the development of Christian doctrine as *profectus fidei non permutatio*. And so as regards the Jewish Law, our Lord said that he came "not to destroy but to fulfill." . . .

When Roman Catholics are accused of substituting another gospel for the primitive creed, they answer that they hold, and can show that they hold, the doctrines of the Incarnation and Atonement as firmly as any Protestant can state them. To this it is replied that they do certainly profess them but that they obscure and virtually annul them by their additions, that the *cultus* of St. Mary and the saints is no development of the truth but a corruption, because it draws away the mind and heart from Christ. They answer that, so far from this, it subserves, illustrates, protects the doctrine of our Lord's condescension and mediation. Thus the parties in controversy join issue on the common ground, that a developed doctrine which reverses the course of development which has preceded it is no true development but a corruption.

A non-Catholic will have difficulty seeing why there should be a "*cultus* of St. Mary." Catholic devotion to the mother of Christ seems an unnecessary addition to "simple Christianity." At best it removes the focus from Jesus; at worst it substitutes veneration of the Mother for adoration of the Son. But Mary-less Christianity collapses into a cold, austere faith in which what Ronald Knox called the "courtesy" of God to man is obscured by his judgment and condemnation of the sinner. It isn't that Christ can't be understood rightly on his own but that, given human nature, few Christians are likely to end up with a right understanding if they don't view him from multiple directions at once, one of them being in parallel with the eyes of his mother. This is something few Protestants grasp until well on their way to the Catholic Church. Almost always Protestants, whether moving toward the Church or recoiling from it, will ask first about Mary. (Next in line: the Inquisition, Galileo, and bad popes and priests.) The problem for the apologist is that an appreciation of Mary comes later, both logically and affectively. Often that appreciation is the last thing a prospective convert acquires. No doubt this delay is a consequence of centuries of anti-Marian propaganda that formed a hereditary prejudice hard—for many, almost impossible—to overcome.

The refutation and remedy of errors cannot precede their rise, and thus the fact of false developments or corruptions involves the correspondent manifestation of true ones. Moreover, all parties appeal to Scripture, that is, argue from Scripture, but argument implies deduction, that is, development. Here there is no difference between early times and late, between a pope *ex cathedra* and an individual Protestant, except that their authority is not on a par. On either side the claim of authority is the same, and the process of development.

Accordingly, the common complaint of Protestants against the Church of Rome is not simply that she has added to the primitive or the scriptural doctrine but that she contradicts it and moreover imposes her additions as fundamental truths under sanction of an anathema. For themselves they deduce by quite as subtle a method, and act upon doctrines as implicit and on reasons as little analysed in time past, as Catholic schoolmen. What small prominence has the Royal Supremacy in the New Testament, or the lawfulness of bearing arms, or the duty of public worship, or the substitution of the first day of the week for the seventh, or infant baptism, to say nothing of the fundamental principle that the Bible and the Bible only is the religion of Protestants! These doctrines and usages, true or not, which is not the question here, are surely gained not by a mere exercise of argument upon words and sentences placed before the eyes but by the unconscious growth of ideas habitual to the mind.

And, indeed, when we turn to the consideration of particular doctrines on which Scripture lays the greatest stress, we shall see that it is absolutely impossible for them to remain in the mere letter of Scripture, if they are to be more than mere words or to convey a definite idea to the recipient. When it is declared that "the Word became flesh," three wide questions open upon us on the very announcement. What is meant by "the Word," what by "flesh," what by "became"? The answers to these involve a process of investigation and are developments. Moreover, when they have been made, they will suggest a series of secondary questions, and thus at length a multitude of propositions is the result, which gather round the inspired sentence of which they come, giving it externally the form of a doctrine and creating or deepening the idea of it in the mind.

As Frank Sheed noted, you can't prevent people from drawing true conclusions from true facts, and you can't prevent them from asking questions. If Christianity remains only at the level of "the mere letter of Scripture," it stifles itself. It becomes like a truncated syllogism that has two premises but a missing conclusion. Any mind not entirely somnolent will want to draw the conclusion—which then becomes the premise in a new syllogism. Often I have been surprised at how rapidly a Protestant controversialist will bring his argument to an artificial halt: this far and no further. He arrives at a proposition that is congenial to him but refuses to see where it leads, perhaps because he fears it will lead too near Catholicism.

Moreover, while it is certain that developments of revelation proceeded all through the Old Dispensation down to the very end of our Lord's ministry, on the other hand, if we turn our attention to the beginnings of apostolical teaching after his Ascension, we shall find ourselves unable to fix an historical point at which the growth of doctrine ceased and the rule of faith was once for all settled. Not on the day of Pentecost, for St. Peter had still to learn at Joppa about the baptism of Cornelius; not at Joppa and Caesarea, for St. Paul had to write his epistles; not on the death of the last apostle, for St. Ignatius [of Antioch] had to establish the doctrine of the episcopacy; not then, nor for many years after, for the canon of the New Testament was still undetermined. Not in the creed, which is no collection of definitions but a summary of certain *credenda*, an incomplete summary and, like the Lord's Prayer or the Decalogue, a mere sample of divine truths, especially of the more elementary. No one doctrine can be named which starts *omnibus numeris* at first and gains nothing for the investigation of faith and the attacks of heresy. The Church went forth from the world in haste, as the Israelites from Egypt "with their dough before it was leavened, their kneading troughs being bound up in the clothes they wore upon their shoulders."

Fundamentalist and Evangelical controversialists happily refer to Scripture to prove their distinctive beliefs, but they don't so much find those beliefs in the sacred text as they retroject them there. Is baptism of infants unwarranted? Many of them say so and cite verses that, they think, support their contention, though those verses easily enough can bear other interpretations. What these controversialists fail to see is that the question of infant baptism was left inchoate in the early Church, at least at the level of positive explication. They take the silence to mean condemnation, but that is a dangerous principle. I sometimes have amused myself by asking them, if they reject infant baptism because the practice is not taught explicitly in the New Testament, on what principle do they accept *sola scriptura*, which has even less warrant in the text. The best they have done is to insist that that isn't the case, at which point they change to a more congenial subject.

No one doubts, with such exception as has just been allowed, that the Roman Catholic communion of this day is the successor and representative of the Medieval Church or that the Medieval Church is the legitimate heir of the Nicene; even allowing that it is a question whether a line cannot be drawn between the Nicene council and the Church which preceded it.

On the whole, all parties will agree that, of all existing systems, the present communion of Rome is the nearest approximation in fact to the Church of the Fathers, possible, though some may think it, to be nearer to it still on paper. Did St. Athanasius or St. Ambrose come suddenly to life, it cannot be doubted what communion they would mistake for their own. All surely will agree that these Fathers, with whatever differences of opinion, whatever protests, if we will, would find themselves more at home with such men as St. Bernard or St. Ignatius Loyola, or with the lonely priest in his lodgings, or the holy sisterhood of mercy, or the unlettered crowd before the altar, than with the rulers or the members of any other religious community.

I sometimes have wondered whether sectarians who imagine a great apostasy occurring around the end of the first century—Mormons, Jehovah's Witnesses, and many Fundamentalists—really believe that their own religion mirrors, in its habits and worship style, the religion of Christianity's first decades. Is there evidence that early Christians practiced baptism for the dead or that they held that Christ died not on a cross but on a stake? Is there evidence the nascent Church in Antioch or Corinth had altar calls? No, Newman is quite right. If Christians from any time within the first millennium appeared on our streets, they would not end up at the local stake, Kingdom Hall, or Good Book Baptist but at the Catholic parish, no matter how fine or egregious its architecture, no matter how welcoming or sullen its congregants.

Those who will not view the beginning in the light of the result are equally unwilling to let the whole elucidate the parts. The Catholic doctrines, as I have already had occasion to observe, are members of one family and suggestive, or correlative, or confirmatory, or illustrative of each other. In other words, one furnishes *evidence* to another, and all to each of them; if this is proved, that becomes probable; if this and that are both probable, but for different reasons, each adds to the other its own probability. The Incarnation is the antecedent of the doctrine of mediation and the archetype both of the sacramental principle and the merit of saints. From the doctrine of mediation follow the Atonement, the Mass, the merits of martyrs and saints, their invocation and *cultus*. From the sacramental principle come the sacraments properly so called; the unity of the Church, and the Holy See as its type and centre; the authority of councils; the sanctity of rites; the veneration of holy places, shrines, images, vessels, furniture, and vestments. Of the sacraments, baptism is developed into confirmation on the one hand; into penance, purgatory, and indulgences on the other; and the Eucharist into the Real Presence, adoration of the Host, resurrection of the body, and the virtue of relics. Again, the doctrine of the sacraments leads to the doctrine of justification, justification to that of original sin, original sin to the merit of Calvary. Nor do these separate developments stand independent of each other, but by cross relations they are connected and grow together while they grow from one. The Mass and the Real Presence are parts of one; their intercessory power, and the purgatorial state, and again the Mass and that state are correlative; celibacy is the characteristic mark of monarchism and the priesthood. You must accept the whole or reject the whole; reduction does but enfeeble, and amputation mutilate. It is trifling to receive all but something which is as integral as any other portion; and, on the other hand, it is a solemn thing to receive any part, for, before you know where you are, you may be carried on by a stern logical necessity to accept the whole.

Moreover, since the doctrines all together make up one integral religion, it follows that several evidences which respectively support these doctrines belong to a whole and must be thrown into a common stock, and all are available in the defence of any. A collection of weak evidences makes up a strong evidence; again, one strong argument imparts cogency to collateral arguments which are in themselves weak.

I always have found these paragraphs to be particularly persuasive. I realize that others will be unmoved by them, but I think that will be out of obstinacy rather than disagreement. There is a kind of circumincession at work in this. Just as the three Persons of the Trinity "coinhere" in one another, so one Christian doctrine fructifies and explicates another, and a proof *here* bolsters a proof *there*. The result is a latticework of belief, each element logically related to the others and each strengthening the edifice.

> When the Church, then, was thrown upon her own resources, first local disturbances gave rise to bishops, and next ecumenical disturbances gave rise to popes; and whether communion with the pope was necessary for Catholicity would not and could not be debated till a suspension of that communion had actually occurred. It is not a greater difficulty that St. Ignatius [of Antioch] does not write to the Asian Greeks about popes than that St. Paul does not write to the Corinthians about bishops. And it is a less difficulty that the papal supremacy was not formally acknowledged in the second century than that there was no formal acknowledgement of the doctrine of the Holy Trinity until the fourth. No doctrine is defined until it is violated. . . .
>
> The fault of [Johann Karl Ludwig] Gieseler [1792–1854, a Protestant church historian], as it seems to me, is his distorting facts to serve a theory; if Catholic controversialists have at any time done the like, they have done what their hypothesis did not require. If the Catholic hypothesis is true, it neither needs nor is benefited by unfairness. Adverse facts should be acknowledged; explained if but apparent; accounted for if real; or let alone and borne patiently as being fewer and lighter than the difficulties of other hypotheses.

It would have been convenient for the Catholic apologist if everything in Catholic history had been tidy, if every pope had been a saint and every Catholic ruler mild and wise. Someone new to apologetics may be tempted to obscure every blemish, but this is imprudent. It just won't work—knowledgeable non-Catholics know too much—and it isn't necessary. The members of the Church are human beings, not angels. Even the wisest and saintliest of them have worked under the effects of original sin. If the Church were a society of the perfect, it would be quite unlike what we have known at any point in history. (It also would be empty.)

Newman here brings up another obvious but often overlooked fact: "No doctrine is defined until it is violated." The late appearance of a formal definition does not imply that the doctrine was a late-appearing novelty. It means that the Church didn't have sufficient motivation to iron out the details. This rankles some people. They think about how much contention could have been avoided had the *Catechism of the Catholic Church* been promulgated under Clement I in 92 rather than under John Paul II in 1992. They might as well wonder why Hammurabi issued his Code instead of anticipating the American Constitution.

> No one will be disposed to deny that the body of doctrine which at this day goes by the name of Catholic is at once the historical and the logical continuation of the body of doctrine so called in the eighteenth, in the seventeenth, in the sixteenth, and so back in every preceding century successively till we come to the first. Whether it be a corrupt development or a legitimate, conducted on sound logic or fallacious, the present so-called Catholic religion is the successor, the representative, and the heir of the religion of the so-called Catholic Church of primitive times.

Newman's methodology in his *Essay* is to work backward through the centuries. He began with the Catholic Church as he knew it. Could this body, with its distinctive beliefs, be found in the eighteenth century? In the seventeenth? In the Reformation era? In the Middle Ages? Working backward Newman could demonstrate the continuity of the Church, even as its outward appearances and devotional emphases changed over time. At no point could one say the Church suddenly sprang up as a distinct offshoot from what before then had been Christianity. At each historical stage there was continuity, not just in the ecclesiastical structure but also in doctrines.

Take any of the early Christian writers—not just the orthodox Fathers of the Church but also those writers who failed to achieve that title because of their own heterodoxy: Origen, for instance, who taught the ultimate emptying of hell, or Tertullian, who ended his life as a Montanist heretic. Bring such men to our own time and ask them to locate the Church and they will point to the Catholic Church, despite obvious but superficial differences from the Church of their own times. No one could imagine Origen or Tertullian, let alone Irenaeus or Augustine or Athanasius, concluding that the Christianity he knew is found today in an Evangelical mega-church or the Kingdom Hall of the Jehovah's Witnesses.

> The use of temples, and these dedicated to particular saints and ornamented on occasions with branches of trees; incense, lamps, and candles; votive offerings on recovery from illness; holy water; asylums; holy-days and seasons, use of calendars, processions, blessings on the fields; sacerdotal vestments, the tonsure, the ring in marriage, turning to the East, images at a later date, perhaps the ecclesiastical chant, and the *Kyrie Eleison*, are all of pagan origin and sanctified by their adoption into the Church.

I have lost count of how many times I have made use of this paragraph when speaking to Fundamentalists—because many of their own controversialists use it, though with a sneaky elision. They use it because Newman admits that the Catholic Church brought in much from paganism, not in terms of belief but at least in terms of custom and practice. These things "are all of pagan origin"—what a self-condemning admission! When I quote the paragraph, I put back in the four-word phrase that commonly is omitted: "the ring in marriage." Nearly all of my Fundamental-ist listeners are married, and nearly all of them received a ring at the marriage ceremony, which means, from their point of view, they adopted a pagan practice. Of course they see no pagan con-notation in wedding rings, and they are right to think that way, though it would be considerate of them if they extended the same principle to Catholics. Never have I met a Fundamentalist who objected to our convention for naming days of the week: Sun Day (in honor of the pagan sun god), Moon Day (after the moon god), Thor's Day (after the Norse god), Saturn's Day (after the Roman god). Sunday, Monday, Thursday, and Saturday—as names for days of the week—long ago lost all pagan meaning, and no Christian fears that by using those names he violates the First Commandment.

> And if we take a survey of Europe at least, we shall find that those religious communions which are characterized by the observance of St. Mary are not the churches that have ceased to adore her eternal Son but such as have renounced that observance. . . . And next it must be asked, whether the character of Protestant devotion toward our Lord has been that of worship at all and not rather such as we pay to an excellent human being, that is, no higher devotion than that which Catholics pay to St. Mary, differing from it, however, in being familiar, rude, and earthly. Carnal minds will ever create a carnal worship for themselves, and to forbid them the service of the saints will have no tendency to teach them the worship of God.

These are points brought up by Newman's American con-temporary Orestes Brownson (1803–1876), like Newman a con-vert. Brownson entered the Church almost exactly one year be-fore Newman did and wrote a book with the now-provocative title *Saint Worship and the Worship of Mary.* In his time, the word *worship* included not just adoration—the meaning to which the word now is restricted—but veneration and honor. Even today

we have the anomaly of certain British magistrates being referred to as "Your Worship," with no one supposing that even
the most servile attorneys give those judges adoration due only
to God. If Brownson's book were to appear today, its title might
be *The Veneration of Mary and the Saints.*

One of his points was that Protestants shy away from venerat-
ing the saints because their own forms of corporate worship fall
short. In the Catholic Mass we find the re-presentation, in an
unbloody form, of the actual sacrifice of Calvary. This sacrifice
is itself the highest possible form of worship. There is no equivalent among most Protestants. The veneration they see Catholics
giving to saints seems uncomfortably like the worship given to
God in Protestant services, at least in its outward forms. Thus
Newman wonders "whether the character of Protestant devotion towards our Lord has been that of worship at all."

21

How the Reformation Happened

Hilaire Belloc

God writes straight with crooked lines, but men write crook-edly with straight lines. They undertake an action that they think will end with a particular result, but in the long run the consequences of their action lie scattered all over the landscape, connected only with a zigzag line that no one could have pre-dicted. "There is a strong tendency towards the error of regard-ing men in the past as aiming at what we *now* know to have been the fruits of their actions," writes Hilaire Belloc, "though they themselves could have had no guess at such results, and though they would have been astonished and even appalled had they been told what the consequences would be. So it was with the men who began the Reformation."

Those men—or at least nearly all of them—thought they were agitating for reform of a Church that had fallen into corruptions, partly in belief but mostly in practice. What they produced was a revolt that introduced its own corruptions, particularly in mat-ters of teaching. It is not likely that the Reformers, at least as they were when they started their attempts at reform, would have recognized themselves in what those reforms looked like one or two centuries later. Henry VIII did not seek a new church. He sought a new wife. He ended his life still devoted to the Mass, still thinking himself a Catholic, but he had set in motion a train of events that resulted in only a shadow of the Mass (and only then in the "high church" segment of the Church of England) and in the portmanteau "Anglo-Catholic," a term that disguised that the English church had ceased to be part of the universal Church.

Belloc considers the English Reformation to be an "accident," a term he uses repeatedly. It was an accident of history that could have gone in entirely different directions at several junctures. If

Mary Tudor had not died early, the old faith likely would have been restored. If Elizabeth I had been the strong figure popular history has portrayed her as being, instead of the weak figure Belloc thinks she was, Thomas Cromwell may not have had as much influence as he had, he being the chief architect of English Protestantism. Far earlier on, if the pope, against his better judgment, had not granted a dispensation for the young Henry to marry his late brother's widow, the initial cause of the English Reformation may never have existed at all.

"If ever there were, in all history, an event not desired by its agents; not understood by those who suffered it; coming by no design, but as the prodigious effect of comparatively small and quite incongruous causes, it was the gradual, mechanical, and disastrous destruction in the English mind of that Faith which had made England." That destruction had immeasurable consequence, says Belloc. "But it is certain that if England had not left the unity of Christendom, that unity would be fully recovered today—and long before today."

Until England broke from unity with the successor of Peter, continues Belloc, the nascent Reformation confined itself to German-speaking areas, where it succeeded in one princedom only to be defeated in the neighboring one. There being no unified German state in those days, and not until more than three centuries later, there was no overarching power that could impose the reforms universally. It is likely that by the end of the sixteenth century the situation in the Germanies would have been settled, with most of the region having returned to unity with Rome. Then, in subsequent years, the remaining regions likely would have come back. So Belloc thinks.

But that return became impossible, for practical purposes, once England defected. Its was the first government of national scope to do so. Even though in those years England was neither the financial nor maritime power it later became, and even though its armies were small compared to those on the Continent, it put enough weight onto the balance to tip things in favor of the Reformation in general. "For want of a nail . . ."

Belloc already had written *The Servile State* (1912) and *Economics for Helen* (1924), so it should have surprised no one that he puts much emphasis on monetary motives for the Reformation. With the dissolution of the monasteries in England, vast sums ended up in the hands of the nobles, who thus acquired a rationale for not wanting to return to the old religion. "God helps those who help themselves" became "God helps those who help themselves to other people's wealth." Belloc sees in this vast transfer of property the thing that prevented the English Reformation from being undone.

He sees something similar working within Calvinism. "If we ask what it was in Calvin's doctrine, apart from the opportuneness of its moment and its effect against the clergy which gave it so much power, the answer is, I think, that it provided an awful [that is, awe-filled] object of worship and that it appealed at the same time to a powerful human appetite which Catholicism opposes. The novel object was an implacable God, that appetite was love of money." It is not money itself but the love of money that is the root of all evil, said St. Paul, who by money meant not just coinage but those temporal things—particularly power—to which money was the entrée. It was money, in Belloc's mind, that made the Reformation permanent.

> The Revolt was originally and essentially a protest against two things: the spiritual power of the clergy; the financial power of the hierarchy and its chief, the pope, and of the monastic orders. These two protests were inextricably mixed because the same man who was offended by exclusive spiritual power was also offended by large revenues drawn from his labor and enjoyed by an institution which in his eyes was no longer fulfilling its function. In other words, the Reformation was originally an anti-clerical movement much more than it was an anti-doctrinal movement, and so far from being a rationalistic movement it led men away from rationalism into the opposite, dependence on text and blind acceptance of merely affirmed, though various, unreasoned doctrines.

To think of the Reformation, particularly in its early years, as exclusively or mainly a movement in belief is to think erroneously. Luther did not begin his break from the Church with the full set of doctrinal errors with which he ended his life. Calvin developed his heretical ideas over time; not all of them were in his mind when he first called for change. The ideas held by Cromwell and Cranmer altered as political and ecclesiastical events altered. The Reformation's Athena did not emerge fully formed from the brow of Zeus. The course of the Reformation would be far easier to understand if it were only a matter of doctrines discarded and doctrines invented.

This has made it difficult for Catholic apologists to deal with Protestant challengers, most of whom know little about the origins of their own religion and most of whom confine themselves to disputations about the meaning of passages of Scripture. (Here I refer to those Protestants for whom Scripture remains important.) These people do not appreciate that their interpretations of Scripture and their overall understanding of Christianity are contingent on historical accidents. If Luther had not suffered from scrupulosity, he likely would not have opposed confession and, consequently, might not have so emphasized, and overemphasized, the abuses of indulgences. If Calvin had not fallen for a wrong understanding of predestination, he would not have constructed a religion that was the direct precursor of Puritanism and the ultimate progenitor even of today's secularism. If Henry had not been such a dissolute and had accepted that his heir would be a daughter rather than a son, the end result would not have been the branch theory of Christianity.

Such historical accidents—things that could have gone one way or another—determined what Protestantism became, and they have made it difficult for Protestants of later times to entertain the idea that the distinctives of their religion may not be integral to Christianity as it came from its Founder but may be later accretions. These historical accidents similarly have made it difficult for Catholic apologists to enter a fruitful discussion about doctrines *per se*, since so many of these doctrines are wrapped up in historical prejudices that have to be set to one side if the doctrines are to be seen in themselves.

How the Reformation Happened was one of several books that impressed upon me the need to deal with non-Catholic claims on multiple levels: doctrinal, philosophical, historical. I found the stories Belloc relates fascinating in themselves—he always is a fine raconteur—and many will read them as they read any other history, but for me their chief utility was in showing how today's non-Catholic, whether Protestant or materialist or whatever, can be approached successfully only if approached widely.

22

A Summary of Catholic History

Newman C. Eberhardt

There are longer histories of the Catholic Church, better known histories, and histories with the standard scholarly apparatus (this one has no citations or footnotes), but it was Newman C. Eberhardt's two-volume set that came into my possession as I began to need to work up responses to historical claims against the Church. His work had sufficient material from which to devise arguments on most disputed points, yet it was not so detailed, or so weighed down with extraneous matter, that I was tempted to set it aside.

Setting it aside would have been unlikely anyway because Eberhardt (1912–1995) wrote well. His style is clean and spare and would not be described as novelistic, as would Belloc's style in his histories. It is a good style, with no padding and no tendentious remarks. Eberhardt, who taught at St. John's Seminary in Camarillo, California, began his preface this way: "Until the appearance of the perfect Church history text, the present summary is offered to assist students in attaining a working knowledge of the subject, intermediate between a brief survey and an exhaustive treatment. . . . While the present work is based upon the most extensive and recent research of which the compiler is capable, it is itself merely a secondary source which must dispense with the apparatus of scholarship."

Referring to himself in the third person, Eberhardt explained that it was

> his aim neither to shy away from scandals nor to feature
> them; to be unashamed of brief references to Providence
> and *corollaria pietatis*, and yet not to moralize. He professes
> no desire to usurp the divine prerogative of judging the

subjective sincerity of Catholic foes, such as the founders of the Oriental and Protestant divisions, but neither does he feel obligated to refrain from criticizing their objective views and conduct, not to place the entire blame on bad Catholics in an effort to be conciliatory. If occasionally well-meaning mistakes of Catholic leaders and saints have been criticized, the compiler professes no neutrality in their regard; these are the stars, these are the heroes of Catholic history by the grace of him who made them saints and leaders and through the intercession of the Queen of Saints.

Looking back now on almost three decades of full-time apologetics, preceded by nearly a decade of part-time work in that vineyard, I am gratified to see how many people have entered work that once was done by so few. Twenty years ago, in a public lecture, a prominent priest-professor chastised "the New Apologists" for being insufficiently subservient to the kind of theologizing he engaged in. Today those New Apologists are no longer young, and they have been joined by Newer Apologists, who in time will be joined by yet another iteration. If my cohort of apologists found it necessary to be jacks of all trades, since they had to handle questions coming from every direction, the maturation of Catholic apologetics has permitted some Newer Apologists to focus on circumscribed issues and thus to work up oral presentations and writings that are more detailed, even if likely to be of use to fewer people. Over time, the result will be a panoply of materials, some broad, others laser-beamed, all aimed at dealing with problems and objections no matter how scattershot or how narrow.

All this is good and necessary. If (lowercased) newer apologists—and here I mean those of my generation and later, as distinguished from the two prior generations that featured Frank Sheed, Arnold Lunn, and so many others—have lacunae, perhaps the most obvious is in the area of Catholic history. Many apologists working today have great facility with scriptural exegesis and scriptural argumentation: they have large swaths of the sacred text memorized (or so it appears to me and to their audiences), they have studied the other side's claims and have found the weak points, and they have succeeded in rescuing the Bible, making it a Catholic book again, in the eyes of their co-religionists. Some apologists have mastered the sects, especially distinctively American sects such as Mormonism and the Jehovah's Witnesses. Others have fine-tuned responses to the secularist attack. For all that, few of today's apologists have the historical depth of those earlier generations. Many seem uninterested in the Christian story past the first century. It is difficult for me to think of any Catholic apologists who are able to relate, even in broad strokes, the history of the papacy from the time of Clement I to Alexander VI, though I can think of a few who have familiarity with popes of the Reformation period onward.

This is a defect. Perhaps it has arisen from having dealt with Protestants too much on their own terms. Do Protestant controversialists accept only the testimony of Scripture? Then we will spar with them exclusively on that level. That should suffice: after all, Scripture, when properly understood, will be seen to bear the Catholic sense, and so the Catholic interpretation will prevail—as, increasingly, it has, as Catholic apologists have honed their skills. Do Protestants have a bifurcated Christian history, one that leaps from the end of the first century to the beginning of the sixteenth? Then we will deal with Christian history, to the extent we deal with it at all (not much), by leaving out the millennium-and-a-half that began with Clement and ended with Alexander.

This way of operation not only concedes too much to the opposition, as though a spiritual and intellectual dark age took up three-quarters of the time since the death of the last apostle, but it deprives the Catholic arsenal of powerful weapons. The Church was established to last to the end of time and thus was established to last through history. At every moment the Church's history can teach us something, not merely through what it teaches overtly in its decrees and catechisms but through what it teaches in the everyday life of its faithful members. Even the unfaithful teach by their examples, as heretics teach by their errors: frequently we learn more from others' foibles than from positive instruction.

Catholic history, despite its ups and downs and persistent confusions and complexities, validates Catholic beliefs, because Catholic history is those beliefs lived out, however ineffectively or haphazardly. It was not until Lateran IV that Christians were given a detailed and definitive understanding of the Real Presence of Christ in the Eucharist, a culminating gloss on John 6. The formal decree of that council was the end of a centuries-long interplay of intellectual forces. If an apologist can establish, in the minds of his hearers or readers, the authority of the Catholic Church and thus the authority of Lateran IV, he has a useful tool when it comes to interpreting John 6. If you acknowledge the authority of the Church *here*, you must acknowledge it *there*.

I am no historian and never have been tempted to become one, but I have been happy to make use of what Catholic historians have served up. With greater or lesser success, and with greater or lesser facility, they have tried to explain what happened and why. Apologists ought to familiarize themselves with the history of the Church because its history is useful in their work—not just in the utilitarian sense of retrojecting a later, definitive interpretation onto first-century understandings but in the practical sense of making what Chesterton called the Catholic Thing come alive for today's Catholics.

23

The Faith of the Early Fathers

William A. Jurgens

Giving a parish seminar in Southern California meant more than just driving to the venue and walking up to the microphone. It meant loading the car with boxes of books to be sold at the literature table. Usually books were chosen to correlate with the theme of the lecture, though a few evergreens came along too. Realizing that most attendees were not regular readers of religious books—or perhaps of any books—I tried to choose works that had attractive covers and that were blessedly short.

This three-volume set by Fr. William A. Jurgens (1928–1982) was neither. The covers featured the poor typography and abstract symbolism for which Liturgical Press was justifiably derided, and the pages not only were oversized, at six-and-a-half by nine-and-a-half inches, but there were more than 1,200 of them. At a time when many books at the table sold for ten dollars, the Jurgens set sold for forty-five. (Today the retail price is around sixty dollars.) There was nothing the least bit attractive about these books in appearance, but I sensed they might prove attractive to prospective buyers if I pitched them properly.

I recall taking thirty shrink-wrapped sets to a seminar near Los Angeles. I chose *The Faith of the Early Fathers* because my talk was on the Catholicity of the early Church. Who better to attest to that than the earliest Christians? The best way to discover what they thought is to read their own words. That is a daunting task in the normal course of things, since it requires reading dozens of thick volumes of the collected works of the Fathers of the Church. How, in that mountain of material, could one track down what the early Christians thought baptism was and did and to whom it licitly could be administered? How could one trace what those early believers believed about the role of bishops as contrasted with the role of priests?

For me Jurgens solved the problem neatly. He went through the whole corpus of patristic writings and selected the most pertinent passages from dozens of writers and hundreds of documents. He arranged them chronologically, starting with the *Didache* and ending with St. John Damascene. He provided information about the writer and key selections from the man's writings. Material from Irenaeus, who wrote in the late second century, is prefaced by two paragraphs about the saint followed by three paragraphs about his best-known work, *Against Heresies*, from which eighteen pages of quotations (seventy quotations in all) are given, followed by two pages of notes by Jurgens.

Each quotation is keyed to a detailed doctrinal index, which is the most valuable attribute of the set. Irenaeus is quoted as saying that "Matthew also issued among the Hebrews a written Gospel in their own language," meaning Aramaic. In the margin is a reference to item 64 in the doctrinal index, where the topic is given as "The authenticity and historicity of the Gospel of Matthew." Fifteen links are given to other works. In a few minutes a reader can review all the relevant ancient writings about the status of the first Gospel.

So I took those thirty sets of Jurgens to that seminar. At the conclusion of my lecture I touted several of the books on the literature table but gave special emphasis to *The Faith of the Early Fathers*. I said that anyone truly interested in what the early Church taught—and how the earliest Christian writings demonstrate that that Church was Catholic—ought to set aside time regularly to see what these ancient documents said. I must have been a good salesman that night. Most of the books on the table sold well, but all copies of the Jurgens set were snatched up, despite the relatively high price. Perhaps no other parish seminar convinced me so much of the intellectual hunger felt by everyday Catholics.

After that, I tried to tout the ancient writers at every opportunity. Sometimes there was immediate gratification. Someone would come up to the table, admit he hadn't heard of the Fathers, and say that he suspected that he would find in Jurgens's pages, or in comparable works, just what he needed to set a friend straight. More often, the gratification was delayed by years.

In 1994 I debated Dave Hunt. That was the year in which his book *A Woman Rides the Beast: The Roman Catholic Church and the Last Days* appeared. Hunt, who died in 2013, claimed that the Catholic Church was the Whore of Babylon, a claim not original to him, of course, but one going back centuries. He just recast the claim in a modern context.

We squared off in a large auditorium in the Detroit area. The audience consisted chiefly of people sympathetic to Hunt's position, though there was a substantial contingent of Catholics. Throughout the debate he and I unsurprisingly disagreed about how the Bible ought to be interpreted. Toward the end of my remarks, I affirmed that people of good will could disagree not just on the sacred text's meaning but on which authorities should be followed in coming to an understanding of that text. On whom should we rely?

Hunt said we should turn to the Reformers to understand what the earliest Christians thought the Bible meant. I suggested that it would make more sense to turn to the early Christians themselves, since the subsequent millennium could have introduced confusions about what the first believers believed. I referred to the Fathers of the Church and particularly to the Apostolic Fathers, those who learned from the apostles themselves. I concluded with a challenge: a listener convinced that the Fathers taught proto-Protestantism had nothing to lose (if he was right) except his illusions (if he was wrong). Reading the Fathers either would affirm the listener's present understanding or would remove him from error. Which would it be?

Some years later I spoke at a conference in another state. During a break between sessions, Catholic apologist Steve Ray introduced me to Alex Jones and said I was responsible for his conversion. I asked Steve what he meant. Jones, who had been the pastor of Pentecostal churches in Detroit, said he had been in the audience when I debated Hunt, with whose position he was largely in agreement. With a smile, he said he found not a single argument I made for the Catholic Church to be convincing, but he was intrigued by the challenge I set out in my final remarks. What harm could come, he thought, from reading the Fathers? They surely would confirm Hunt's position and his own, and reading them would be further proof that the Catholic Church and its advocates had had things wrong from the first.

The Fathers spelled the end of Jones's Protestantism because he realized, to his dismay, that they were Catholic. The more he read them, the less his Protestant positions seem defensible. The more he read them, the more he realized that Hunt had mischaracterized Catholicism grotesquely, as had other anti-Catholic writers. Over a course of years, and while his own thinking was in flux, Jones, who died in 2017, introduced Catholic practices and teachings into his church. When he finally converted, he brought much of his flock with him.

24

Patrology

Johannes Quasten

At the southernmost tip of the seaside town of San Clemente, California is Casa Pacifica, which was known during Richard Nixon's presidency as the Western White House. Casa Pacifica is of historical interest, but there is something nearby that always has been of greater interest to me. Three miles north along Interstate 5 is what surely must be the most ecumenically-minded Presbyterian church in the country. I call it that because San Clemente Presbyterian Church is named, almost unavoidably, after the fourth pope, Clement of Rome, who died around the year 100. Each time I drive by I smile at the incongruity of the church's name, which appears in large letters facing the freeway. Presbyterians never have been known as defenders of papal prerogatives, so it is pleasant to see them, even inadvertently, making a pro-papal gesture.

The Clement whose name is now enshrined midway between Los Angeles and San Diego was one of the Apostolic Fathers. The term means a Father of the Church who learned from the apostles themselves. (Tertullian claimed that Clement was consecrated a bishop by Peter.) It is from the Fathers of the Church and from other early writers and writings that we discover what the earliest Christians believed and how they lived. The New Testament tells us little about even the earliest days of the Church and, of course, nothing about what occurred after the sacred books were written. The New Testament has been sufficiently imprecise that, over the centuries, people of intelligence and good will have drawn countless contradictory interpretations from it. The fourth evangelist, John, said that not all that Jesus taught was written down and, hyperbolically, that he taught so much that not even all the books of the world could contain his teachings. Most of those teachings had to be passed along in some manner other than on the pages of Scripture itself.

This brings us to the writings of the first few Christian centuries. It is in those writings that we see the first understandings reduced to paper. It is in them that we discover what the earliest Christians understood Christianity to be. Not that they always were in accord. Often enough there were conflicting interpretations, some merely differences at the level of nuance, others entirely opposite one another. For the most part, though, we find remarkable consistency, and we see even in those centuries a separation of the wheat and chaff, with not a few early writers being declared unorthodox by the Church.

Much of the allure of the Gospels comes from their being in part biographical and in part doctrinal. Reading them, we learn who Christ was and what he taught. Similarly with patrology, which is the study of the Fathers of the Church (and of certain other writers not eligible for that title) with regard not just to the teachings they passed along but to their own histories as writers and public figures. Patrology thus combines both biography and theology, a combination I always have found attractive. *The City of God* appeals not just because of its content but because we know of its author through his *Confessions*.

"Patrology is that part of the history of Christian literature which deals with the theological authors of Christian antiquity," explains Johannes Quasten (1900–1987) in his introduction. Patrology "comprises both the orthodox and the heretical writers, although it treats with preference those authors who represent the traditional ecclesiastical doctrine, the so-called Fathers and Doctors of the Church. Thus, patrology can be defined as the science of the Fathers of the Church." The years covered differ between the West and the East. In the West, patrology includes writers through Gregory the Great, who died in 604. In the East, it includes writers through John Damascene, who died in 749.

In Quasten's explanation there lurks an ambiguity. He says that, on the one hand, patrology deals with both the orthodox and the heterodox. Since the word *patrology* has its root in *pater* (father), one might conclude that even the heterodox are to be considered Fathers of the Church. Not so. That title is reserved for the orthodox. An ancient writer such as Tertullian, who began writing as an orthodox Catholic but ended his writing career as a heretic (a Montanist), is just that—an ancient writer. Justin Martyr was more than just an ancient writer; thoroughly orthodox, he also was a Father of the Church, and he happened to be the first Catholic apologist.

Quasten notes that "only those are to be regarded as 'Fathers of the Church' who combine these four necessary qualifications: orthodoxy of doctrine, holiness of life, ecclesiastical approval, and antiquity." There is a further designation that overlaps with "Father of the Church": "Doctor of the Church." Half of the latter lived in the second Christian millennium, but they all share the four notes Quasten mentions. In addition, Doctors of the Church have two other notes: "eminent erudition" and the express declaration of the Church that they are to be considered Doctors. Eight of the earliest are singled out, four from the West and four from the East: in the West, Ambrose, Jerome, Augustine, and Gregory the Great; in the East, Basil, Gregory of Nazianzus, John Chrysostom, and Athanasius.

Let's return to Clement of Rome. He is the first of the Apostolic Fathers considered by Quasten, who devotes twenty-one pages to him. First comes a biographical overview, necessarily brief because so little is known about Clement. Irenaeus said that Clement knew both Peter and Paul, and Eusebius—the first important writer of ecclesiastical history—identified him with the Clement who is mentioned in the Epistle to the Philippians. Less likely is the identification of Clement as the Roman consul Titus Flavius Clemens, who was executed around A.D. 96 for being a Christian.

We have only one writing that indisputably is from Clement, his *Letter to the Corinthians*. Quasten says that this is "the earliest piece of Christian literature outside the New Testament for which the name, position, and date of the author are historically attested." This document is important for multiple reasons. It corroborates Peter's trip to Rome and Paul's to Spain, and it recounts the martyrdom of those two apostles in Rome. More importantly, it shows that the bishop of Rome, Clement, takes up the resolution of a dispute occurring in Corinth—the first example we have of papal authority extending to the universal Church in post-apostolic times.

After devoting several pages to a consideration of the content of Clement's letter, Quasten discusses its time of composition, how the author's personality is manifested in the text, and the history of the text's transmission. Many citations are given. After that Quasten examines documents that are said to be from Clement's hand but probably were not, such as a so-called *Second Letter*.

What the reader is given, throughout Quasten's three volumes, largely corresponds to what is given for Clement: the man's biographical information (often sketchy, given that in ancient times there were no biographies in the modern sense of the term); an overview of the chief writings, both assuredly his and those only attributed to him; consideration of the chief theological and historical points in the writings; and a situating of the writer among other writers of his time. What Quasten does is different from what Joseph Tixeront does in his *History of Dogmas*. One follows the writers through history, the other follows the ideas. There necessarily is overlap, and Quasten and Tixeront illuminate each other. It is as though one writer of musicology focused on the composers of an era while another writer focused on the musical styles of the same period. One writer worked from a consideration of the life of Bach, while another worked from a consideration of his fugues and partitas. One approach magnified the other.

25

History of Dogmas

Joseph Tixeront

I consider this the companion set to Johannes Quasten's *Patrology*, even though the books were written forty-six years apart and in different countries. The two sets have been neighbors on my shelves for more than thirty years. I have been unable to think of one without thinking of the other, unable to dip into one without looking up parallel material in the other.

Joseph Tixeront (1856–1925) was a Sulpician theologian and patrologist. In the preface he writes that "the work was intended to be complete in one volume," but apparently things got out of hand. All he was able to handle in the first volume was ante-Nicene theology—that is, theology as it developed prior to the Council of Nicaea, which was held in 325. I surmise that he intended to wrap up his project in a second volume but in the process discovered he was unable to do so. In the second volume he covered developments from Athanasius to Augustine. It required a third volume to bring his study up to the end of the patristic age. I know the feeling.

My first substantial foray into apologetical writing was in the pages of *The Wanderer*, a Catholic weekly newspaper. After having dabbled in apologetics on a small scale for several years, I proposed to the editor a short series on the Fundamentalist challenge to the Church. I guessed that three weekly installments of about 3,000 words apiece would be enough to cover the subject adequately. Always in need of copy, *The Wanderer* happily agreed to my proposal.

By the time I completed the first installment, I realized that I had underestimated the task. Would the editor consent to my expanding the series to five installments? Certainly, he replied. We can make accommodations. By the time I had written two or three more weekly pieces I saw that I still had far to go. The more I re-searched, the more I found worth writing about. I had begun with a list of anti-Catholic charges and anti-Catholic writers, and as I covered them I learned of still more charges and writers. It seemed that I would require eight installments rather than just five.

So it went, week after laborious week. As soon as I sent off one installment, I began research for the next. After research came writing. After writing came editing. After editing came the dis-satisfaction of another looming weekly deadline. The more I wrote, the more needed to be written. The horizon moved ever further from me. I caught up to it less because I ran out of things to say than because I was on the verge of exhaustion.

The three-part series ended up having thirty parts. They were the first drafts (and, in most cases, the final drafts, since I had edited them carefully) of the chapters of what turned out to be my first book, *Catholicism and Fundamentalism*. I wonder now whether I would have ventured on the project had I known the toll it would take, having to meet weekly deadlines while otherwise working at a job full time. Though I wrote out of my home, I suppose my wife often felt like a widow.

That would not have been the case with Joseph Tixeront—cer-tainly not the widow part, since he was a priest—but it appears that he, too, was blindsided by his project. What he thought could be handled happily in one volume required three, and I would not be surprised to learn that in his private papers he confessed that, at some point during the project, he feared that, to do the thing justice, he would have to write several additional volumes.

Tixeront begins, appropriately enough, with a definition: "A dogma is, then, a truth revealed [this is the key word], and defined as such by the Church, a truth which the faith of the Christian is obliged to accept." Dogmas are to be distinguished from rules of morality. Gregory of Nyssa said, "Christ divides the Christian discipline into two: the part referring to morals, and that referring to the exactness of dogmas."

Then comes a further distinction, between patrology and pa-tristics. "Both," says Tixeront, "refer exclusively to those writers we call the Fathers of the Church. The former studies their lives and draws up the catalogue, sifts the authenticity and mentions the editions of their works, which, in a word, it considers chiefly from the outside; patristics examines and exposes their doctrine and reveals the treasures contained in them. Both are needed for the history of dogmas."

Quasten's *Patrology* deals, naturally enough, with patrology, although there is patristics in it too: much consideration of what the Fathers taught, not just consideration of their own history and the history of their writings. Tixeront overlaps somewhat with Quasten; he, too, for example, gives an overview of what is known of Clement of Rome, though his treatment is more cursory. Tixeront focuses less on the men than on their thought, less on how their writings came to be than on how what was contained in those writings came to be believed.

The Fathers of the Church—those men who are the object of patrological study—were by definition orthodox. Usually, in discussing them, writers such as Quasten necessarily find themselves mentioning heterodox writers also, since the orthodox writers honed their expressions through interplay with those who fell into heresy. Such men, nevertheless, are secondary or even tertiary characters in patrology. Not so in the historical development of dogmas.

Tixeront devotes considerable space to the earliest heresies, beginning with the end of the first century, which is when they first began to appear with substantial influence. He discusses the Judaizers, the Gnostics, the Nicolaitans, and Cerinthus. The latter was at his most influential at the very end of the apostle John's life. Irenaeus recounts a story told by Polycarp, who had learned at the feet of John. One day John and his disciples were at a public bath house. On being informed that Cerinthus was inside, John said, "Let us flee, lest the building fall down, for Cerinthus, the enemy of the truth, is inside!"

Throughout his three volumes Tixeront demonstrates how the Church's theological sword was sharpened against the whetstone of the heretics. Sometimes people ask why the Church didn't lay out, in great detail, all its dogmas at the beginning, producing a full conspectus of the faith in Year One. That prospect has an obvious attraction—it seems as though many troubles could have been avoided had everything been spelled out from the beginning—but that was not part of the economy of salvation.

The Church's understanding of the truths of which it is the custodian has been one of slow manifestation. With few exceptions, doctrines have not been defined until they have been challenged. The Church has been a preserver, not an innovator—not even an innovator in the sense of trying to keep a few steps ahead of likely opponents. Transubstantiation was not defined, and that theological term of art was not chosen, until after the second Christian millennium had dawned. It was only with the denial of the Real Presence by Berengarius of Tours (999–1088) that the teaching was formalized. Not only was there no perceived need to work out the theology before the eleventh century, but there may not have been, in practical terms, a way to do so without facing the challenge of heresy. Iron sharpens iron, and heresy sharpens orthodoxy.

When I was composing those thirty installments that ended up being *Catholicism and Fundamentalism*, I knew that I would have to frame my arguments in terms that opponents of the Church would accept, even if they never ended up accepting my conclusions. I knew I could not appeal to the authority of popes or councils, because Fundamentalists did not recognize their authority. I realized that they accepted the authority of Scripture, so my series ended up discussing more than 300 passages from the Bible, but I also realized that, at least to some extent, they accepted two other "authorities": history and common sense. I made much use of each of these as I argued the Catholic position.

This is not to say that I expected that my Fundamentalist readers—or my Catholic readers, for that matter—would have much background in Christian history. In fact, I presumed they did not and that, for Fundamentalists, Christian history existed for only a few decades in the first century and then, mysteriously, disappeared for another fourteen centuries, to reappear only when the 95 Theses were posted on the church door in Wittenberg. Between the death of John and the rise of Luther there was a historical black hole. It was my goal to show otherwise.

I counted on the fact that most people like history, once they are introduced to it, and that most people know at least some secular history. Nearly everyone likes stories. Christian history is the story of the Church: its trials, its growth, its heroes, its villains. Unlike the "history" in fiction, real history is true—or at least attempts to be an approximation of the truth. Caesar was assassinated in 44 B.C. The Turks were defeated at Vienna in 1683. Napoleon lost at Waterloo in 1815. These things happened, and they had consequences. So with Church history.

That history can be examined through various lenses. There is the history of the papacy, the history of Christian political entities, the history of dogmas. The categories are many, and, for me, the last often has seemed the most useful because it deals with Christians' attempts to work out the intellectual component of their faith. That working out continues in our own time, but I constantly have been drawn back to the earliest years, those covered by Tixeront and Quasten, since they remain the basis of all that followed.

Envoi

I don't remember ever not being a reader. How that came to be I can't say. Long before Grandma came to visit I habitually ensconced myself with books. I found in them comfort and marvel, wonderment and refuge. I wasn't raised in a bookish family. When I was a young boy, our home had few books and no dedicated bookcase. Later came an encyclopedia purchased serially, month by month, at the supermarket (we couldn't afford the *Encyclopedia Americana*). At some point I ceased spending my allowance on Matchbox cars and started building my own library. I discovered Edgar Rice Burroughs, eventually collecting dozens of his books, two or three of which I have kept as mementos of a youth not ill spent but perhaps too introspective. I went on to other authors then popular with boys and graduated from them to more substantial but equally delightful works, turning my focus from fiction to mathematics, history, theology, and other areas.

In college I wrote my first book, never published. I still have the typescript. When, at long intervals, I peek at it, I see my present self in more than outline. That book will remain forever out of print, as will others I have longed to write but will not be granted time for. I happily would forego the temporary immortality such books could bring if these pages could resuscitate works that made my apologetics career possible, useful, and enjoyable.

These are the twenty-five books discussed in these pages. They are listed in the editions I used when learning to become an apologist. Most remain in print or are available in newer editions, but some have been out of print for decades.

Attwater, Donald, ed., *A Catholic Dictionary*
(New York: Macmillan, 1949), 552 pages.

Attwater, Donald, *A Dictionary of the Popes*
(London: Catholic Book Club, 1939), 337 pages.

Belloc, Hilaire, *How the Reformation Happened*
(New York: Dodd, Mead & Company, 1928), 290 pages.

Belloc, Hilaire, *Survivals and New Arrivals*
(New York: Macmillan, 1930), 219 pages.

Butler, B.C., *The Church and Infallibility*
(London: Catholic Book Club, 1954), 230 pages.

Cozens, Luisa, *A Handbook of Heresies*
(London: Sheed and Ward, 1974 [1928]), 95 pages.

Eberhardt, Newman C., *A Summary of Catholic History*
(St. Louis: Herder, 1961), 2 vols., 1,790 pages.

Halligan, Nicholas, *The Sacraments and Their Celebration*
(New York: Alba House, 1986), 284 pages.

Jurgens, William A., *The Faith of the Early Fathers*
(Collegeville: Liturgical Press, 1970, 1979), 3 vols., 1,240 pages.

Knox, Ronald and Arnold Lunn, *Difficulties*
(London: Eyre & Spottiswoode, 1952 [1932]), 274 pages.

Lunn, Arnold and C.E.M. Joad, *Is Christianity True?*
(Philadelphia: Lippincott, 1933), 386 pages.

Lunn, Arnold, *The Third Day*
(London: Burns Oates, 1945), 145 pages.

O'Brien, John A., ed., *Winning Converts*
(New York: P.J. Kenedy, 1948), 248 pages.

Most, William G., *Catholic Apologetics Today*
(Rockford, Illinois: TAN Books, 1986), 272 pages.

Most, William G., *Free From All Error*
(Libertyville, Illinois: Franciscan Marytown Press, 1985),
179 pages.

Newman, John Henry,
An Essay on the Development of Christian Doctrine
(Baltimore: Penguin, 1974), 449 pages.

Ott, Ludwig, *Fundamentals of Catholic Dogma*
(Cork: Mercier Press, 1955), 544 pages.

Quasten, Johannes, *Patrology*
(Westminster, Maryland: Christian Classics, 1983 [1950]),
3 vols., 1,455 pages.

Rumble, Leslie, and Charles M. Carty, *Radio Replies*
(St. Paul, Minnesota: Radio Replies Press, 1938),
3 vols., 1,046 pages.

Sheed, Frank, *Faith Comes by Hearing*
(London: Sheed and Ward, 1967), 186 pages.

Sheed, Frank, *Theology and Sanity*
(Huntington, Indiana: Our Sunday Visitor, 1978), 331 pages.

Sheed, Frank, *Theology for Beginners*
(New York: Sheed and Ward, 1957), 252 pages.

Thurston, Herbert, S.J.,
No Popery: Chapters on Anti-Papal Prejudice
(London: Sheed and Ward, 1930), 319 pages.

Tixeront, Joseph, *History of Dogmas*
(Westminster, Maryland: Christian Classics, 1984 [1904]),
3 vols., 1,550 pages.

Ward, Maisie and Frank Sheed,
Catholic Evidence Training Outlines, 2nd ed.
(London: Sheed and Ward, 1948), 357 pages.

ABOUT THE AUTHOR

Karl Keating has been a Catholic apologist for four decades and is the founder of Catholic Answers. Among his books are *Catholicism and Fundamentalism*, *The New Geocentrists*, and the *Debating Catholicism* series. For amusement he hikes the peaks of the Sierra Nevada and the depths of the Grand Canyon.